TH
LI
SERIES

GUIDE FOR
LECTORS AND READERS

SECOND EDITION

Michael Cameron

Corinna Laughlin

Virginia Meagher

Paul Turner

LITURGY
TRAINING
PUBLICATIONS

Nihil Obstat
Rev. Mr. Daniel G. Welter, JD
Chancellor
Archdiocese of Chicago
February 26, 2021

Imprimatur
Most Rev. Robert G. Casey
Vicar General
Archdiocese of Chicago
February 26, 2021

The *Nihil Obstat* and *Imprimatur* are declarations that the material is free from doctrinal or moral error, and thus is granted permission to publish in accordance with c. 827. No legal responsibility is assumed by the grant of this permission. No implication is contained herein that those who have granted the *Nihil Obstat* and *Imprimatur* agree with the content, opinions, or statements expressed.

GUIDE FOR LECTORS AND READERS, SECOND EDITION © 2021 Archdiocese of Chicago: Liturgy Training Publications, 3949 South Racine Avenue, Chicago IL 60609; 800-933-1800; fax: 800-933-7094; email: orders@ltp.org; website: www.LTP.org. All rights reserved.

The first edition of this book was titled *Guide for Lectors.*

This book is part of the Liturgical Ministry Series®.

This book was edited by Lorie Simmons. Víctor R. Pérez was the production editor, Anna Manhart was the designer, and Kari Nicholls was the production artist.

25 24 23 22 21   1 2 3 4 5

Printed in the United States of America

Library of Congress Control Number: 2020936477

ISBN: 978-1-61671-578-6

ELLEC2

Contents

Preface   iv

How to Use This Resource   vii

Chapter One
Your Ministry and the Liturgy   1

Chapter Two
The Meaning and History
of Your Ministry   6

Chapter Three
Serving as a Reader   16

Chapter Four
Spirituality and Discipleship   48

Chapter Five
Frequently Asked Questions   58

Resources   62

Glossary   68

Prayer for Readers   71

Preface

The Spirit of the Lord is upon me,
because he has anointed me
to bring glad tidings to the poor.
He has sent me to proclaim liberty to captives
and recovery of sight to the blind,
To let the oppressed go free,
and to proclaim a year acceptable to the Lord.

—Luke 4:18–19

"The Spirit of the Lord is upon me,"[1] Jesus read. He was reading out loud in front of his boyhood neighbors at a synagogue service one Sabbath. Now he was an adult. "The Spirit of the Lord . . . has anointed me,"[2] he continued. People started to pay a little more attention.

Jesus had grown up as any child did. He lived at home. He had friends. He played in the streets. He washed his hands before dinner. The neighbors watched his parents age, and they witnessed his growth in wisdom and grace. One day he left on a spiritual quest. He approached John the Baptist, a charismatic figure with a band of disciples. Jesus surprised John by asking to be baptized, and John agreed. Coming up from the waters, he walked into the desert, where he spent forty days fasting, praying, and overcoming temptation. Now it was time to go to work.

"The Spirit of the Lord . . . has anointed me / to bring glad tidings to the poor,"[3] Jesus read. People listened even more closely. They had been talking about him ever since he returned to Galilee.

Jesus had already preached in nearby towns, but now he was back home in Nazareth. He was walking the streets of his old neighborhood, seeing familiar faces and summoning up memories. This particular day was the Sabbath. He did something he was accustomed to do: he showed up at the synagogue. His neighbors were excited to see him there. They knew of his growing reputation as a spiritual leader, so they asked him to do what he used to do: read the Scripture for the day.

So here is Jesus—the Word of God made flesh. An attendant reaches over and hands him the Word of God on parchment. Jesus picks up the scroll. He unfurls it. He finds the passage he wants. He reads with a voice that would

---

1. Luke 4:18.
2. Luke 4:18.
3. Luke 4:18.

rivet individuals and large throngs: "The Spirit of the Lord is upon me, / because he has anointed me / to bring glad tidings to the poor."[4]

He improvises. He is reading Isaiah 61:1–3, but he interpolates some of Isaiah 58:6, rearranges parts, and adds a thought. He seems to have something very specific in mind. Jesus reads: "He has sent me to proclaim liberty to captives / and recovery of sight to the blind, / to let the oppressed go free, / and to proclaim a year acceptable to the Lord."[5]

His words caught the attention of everyone in the room. They no longer looked at the wall, their sandals, the ceiling, or the floor. They all turned their eyes toward Jesus. Something was happening. They were listening to the Word of God read by the Word of God. They were listening to God.

The message was unmistakable. Hundreds of years prior, through the mouth of Isaiah, God had promised a new kind of liberation; now that promise was being heard—and fulfilled—in their midst.

After reading these few words, Jesus rolled up the scroll, handed it back to the attendant, and took his seat. The worshippers all stared at him. His words hung like humidity in the room.

Then he gave one of the shortest and most powerful homilies ever: "Today this Scripture passage is fulfilled in your hearing."[6]

This story took place in a remote synagogue long ago, but it still transmits an eternal message about who Jesus is, and what the Word of God is.

"The word of God is living and effective," the letter to the Hebrews says, "sharper than any two-edged sword, penetrating even between soul and spirit, joints and marrow, and able to discern reflections and thoughts of the heart."[7]

When we pick up the Word of God, we hold a powerful tool.

The story of Jesus in the synagogue also says something about the role of the reader. As a reader, Jesus had made the Word of God part of his life. He was familiar with the Scriptures. He had absorbed their thoughts into his own.

Jesus was a member of a community. People knew him as a child, and had followed his interests as an adult. Those who attended the synagogue service knew who he was as a person, and also as a minister. They knew he was a reader.

The synagogue service made space for the Word of God. It relied not just on the written word, but also on the spoken word. Worship included the reading of God's Word out loud.

The synagogue reader fulfilled this role in relationship with others. As a reader, Jesus interacted with one other minister, the attendant who handed him the scroll and later took it back. It seems like a small matter, but Jesus had to know the responsibilities of others in order to fulfill his own properly.

---

4. Luke 4:18.
5. Luke 4:18–19.
6. Luke 4:21.
7. Hebrews 4:12.

When Jesus finally proclaimed the reading, he spoke with the voice of God. He engaged his hearers. He knew what the message was and why it was important. He could apply it to the revelation unfolding in the presence of them all. He had perfectly integrated his being, his community, the synagogue, the role of the reader, and the proclamation of the reading. That is what readers still aspire to do.

At Sunday Mass, Christians gather because we also honor the Word of God. As we assemble to celebrate the Eucharist, we do not approach the table of Communion until we have feasted at the table of the Word.

"The Mass consists in some sense of two parts, namely the Liturgy of the Word and the Liturgy of the Eucharist, these being so closely interconnected that they form but one single act of worship. For in the Mass is spread the table both of God's Word and of the Body of Christ, and from it the faithful are to be instructed and refreshed."[8]

In the Scriptures, God speaks to us. At Mass, God speaks to a particular people gathered at a particular time in a particular place. The Word will affect us in different ways. Each person will hear the message uniquely, as the Holy Spirit reaches into the hearts of us all to place within them the message that comes from God.

To work this miracle, God chooses instruments. God uses readers.

A reader integrates many values. Readers are people of faith who have nurtured a relationship with God and have formed their lives on the Gospel. They are members of a community of family, friends, and strangers, bound together by a desire to live near and for one another, and to share opportunities for faith and worship. Readers have come to value their local Church and its mission. They understand the importance of making Sunday worship the highlight of their week. And they strive to make the reading of the Scriptures a highlight of the Mass—because it is.

Readers have personally encountered the Word of God, and through them the People of God encounter the divine Word.

---

8. *General Instruction of the Roman Missal* (GIRM), 28.

How to Use This Resource

You have agreed to serve the Church as a proclaimer of the Word. Both the ordained and the laity, both men and women may be trained to proclaim Scripture at Mass. Technically, the term "lector" refers to a lay reader who has been "instituted," but in North America, lay readers are far more customary than instituted lectors. You will read more about the history of instituted lectors in chapter 2. Although proclaimers of the Word are popularly known both as lectors and readers, this book will generally use the term "reader." As a reader, you will be entrusted with the Word of God—a tool sharper than any two-edged sword. As any skilled craftsman does, you will want to know your tools in order to execute your art well.

The introduction to the *Lectionary for Mass* calls for readers to be given, above all, a spiritual preparation for proclaiming the Word of God. That spiritual preparation should include formation in the liturgy and in the Bible. In addition, the introduction calls for a technical preparation that gives readers skills for reading publicly. This book will prepare you in all of those areas. It will explain the significance of the Word of God and the role of the reader in the liturgy. It will describe how to prepare for and fulfill your duties. It will answer some of the most frequently asked questions about the ministry. And it will invite you into a deeper experience of God through the Bible.

In the absence of an instituted lector, other lay people may be deputed to proclaim the readings from Sacred Scripture, people who are truly suited to carrying out this function and carefully prepared, so that by their hearing the readings from the sacred texts the faithful may conceive in their hearts a sweet and living affection for Sacred Scripture.

—*General Instruction of the Roman Missal*, 101.

The Spirit of God came upon Jesus in a very special way. When he read that passage from Isaiah long ago, he absorbed its meaning as no other reader ever could or ever will. However, the Spirit of God is also upon you. God has placed the Spirit within you, a Holy Spirit who speaks to you, a Holy Spirit who uses you to proclaim the Word of God.

About the Authors

Michael Cameron contributed to chapter 3, including the section on the Bible. He teaches and writes about Scripture and the history of Christianity at the University of Portland in Oregon, holding a PHD in historical theology from the University of Chicago. He also writes pastoral resources (*Unfolding Sacred*

Scripture: How Catholics Read the Bible, LTP) and gives parish workshops and presentations. For many years he has been a reader and trainer of readers.

Corinna Laughlin wrote chapter 1. She is the pastoral assistant for liturgy at St. James Cathedral in Seattle, Washington, and liturgy consultant for the Archdiocese of Seattle. She has written extensively on the liturgy for Liturgy Training Publications, an agency of the Archdiocese of Chicago, and has contributed articles to *Pastoral Liturgy*®, *Ministry and Liturgy*, and other publications. She holds a doctorate in English from the University of Washington.

Virginia Meagher contributed much to chapter 3, Resources, and the Glossary. She has a BS in communication studies from Northwestern University, has done graduate studies in ministry at Loyola University, Chicago, and has worked in parish and diocesan liturgy for many years, including in the Archdiocese of Chicago and the Diocese of Stockton in California. Currently she directs liturgy and music in her parish in the Diocese of Oakland.

Paul Turner wrote the preface and chapters 2 and 4. He is the pastor of the Cathedral of the Immaculate Conception in Kansas City, Missouri, and the director of the Office of Divine Worship for the Diocese of Kansas City–St. Joseph. He holds a doctorate in sacred theology from Sant'Anselmo in Rome and is the author of many pastoral and theological resources. He serves as a facilitator for the International Commission on English in the Liturgy.

Questions for Discussion and Reflection

1. Why have you agreed to serve as a reader? How did God's call come to you?

2. How do you hope to grow from this ministry? (in your understanding of the liturgy, of Scripture, of your own spirituality?)

Chapter One

Your Ministry and the Liturgy

The liturgy is the source and summit of the Christian life.

—*Lumen gentium*, 11

Y ou're reading this book because you're thinking about becoming a proclaimer of the Word in your parish. Or perhaps you already serve in this
way and are looking for an update or refresher. One thing is certain: you're
reading this book because liturgy matters to you.

What Is Liturgy?

Dictionaries will tell you, in one way or another, that *liturgy* is a collection of
rites used in public worship. And that is true. But there is much more to liturgy
than that. The word *liturgy* comes from a Greek word meaning "public work"
or "work of the people." That hits nearer the mark: liturgy is a special kind of
work in which the divine and human come together; we do something, and,
more importantly, God does something. Liturgy is not a thing; liturgy is an
event. So let's ask a different question: What does liturgy *do*?

Liturgy gathers us in the presence of God. In speaking of the
Eucharist, the second-century *Didache* emphasizes gathering: "Even as this
broken bread was scattered over the hills, and was gathered together and
became one, so let Your Church be gathered together
from the ends of the earth into Your kingdom."[1]
Here the eucharistic bread, formed from many
grains of wheat, is an image of what we are to be:
disparate individuals who become something new—
a worshiping assembly. In the Bible, the gathering
of God's people is a sign of the in-breaking of the
kingdom of God. Think of Isaiah's vision of a great
banquet on a mountaintop.[2] Think of Jesus feeding the multitudes[3] or of the
disciples gathered in prayer in the upper room on the first Pentecost.[4] When
God gathers his people together, something happens. The same is true of the
liturgy. Before a word has been spoken or a note sung, the liturgy is already a
sign of the kingdom of God because it gathers us together.

> In the liturgy, by means of
> signs perceptible to the
> senses human sanctification
> is signified and brought
> about in ways proper to
> these signs.
>
> —*Sacrosanctum concilium*, 7

---

1. *The Didache: The Lord's Teaching Through the Twelve Apostles to the Nations*, 9. http://www.new
advent.org/fathers/0714.htm; accessed August 28, 2019.
2. See Isaiah 25:6–9.
3. See Matthew 14:13–21, Mark 6:30-44, Luke 9:10–17, and John 6:1–15.
4. See Acts of the Apostles 2:1–11.

Liturgy helps form us into a community. The act of being together at table, of sharing the Word of God, of being one voice in our sung and spoken prayers, has an impact on us. It is through this shared action in the liturgy that we learn to recognize ourselves as a family of believers, the Body of Christ, and to be united in our action outside of the Church as well. We join in the liturgy because we are a community, but the reverse is also true: without the liturgy, we are not a community at all.

Liturgy is both common and cosmic. The liturgy takes the most ordinary things—our bodies and voices, light and darkness, water and fire, bread, wine, and oil, time itself—and, through the action of the Holy Spirit, transforms all of these into God's very presence. The liturgy teaches us to see that the entire universe is marked with the presence of Christ. The "seeds" of God are everywhere in the world. The stuff of our holiness is not far away, remote, or arcane. The common is holy.

Christian liturgy is always about the paschal mystery. At the heart of all Christian prayer is the paschal mystery—that is, the life, death, and resurrection of Christ. Whether our prayer is the Mass, the Liturgy of the Hours, a saint's day, a sacrament—whether it is Advent or Christmas Time, Lent, Triduum, or Easter Time—the liturgy is always about the paschal mystery. Why is the paschal mystery so important? Because, in the words of St. Paul, "if Christ has not been raised, your faith is vain; you are still in your sins."[5] The paschal mystery is the fulcrum of history and the dynamic reality which gives meaning to our lives and enlivens our worship. We gather for liturgy in order to be plunged, again and again, into the paschal mystery.

In the liturgy, we meet Christ. We know that Christ is always close to those who believe: Jesus said, "whoever loves me will keep my word, and my Father will love him, and we will come to him and make our dwelling with him."[6] But, in the celebration of the Eucharist, Christ is present to us in a special way. In fact, the Church highlights *four* presences of Christ at Mass. Christ is present in the community gathered for prayer; Christ comes to us in each other. Christ is present in the priest, who acts *in persona Christi*, in the person of Christ, in the Mass. Christ is present in the Word proclaimed: "When the Sacred Scriptures are read in the Church, God himself speaks to his people, and Christ, present in his word, proclaims the Gospel."[7] And in a unique way, Christ is present in the consecrated bread and wine, his true Body and Blood, shared with us in the Eucharist. Through our participation in this mystery, we meet Christ in many ways and we become what we receive: the Body of Christ.[8]

---

5. I Corinthians 15:17.
6. John 14:23.
7. GIRM, 29.
8. See *Sacrosanctum concilium*, 7.

Liturgy is the worship of the Church. The liturgy is not free-form. As the official prayer of the universal Church, it is governed by universal norms. Most of the texts we hear at Mass—with some significant exceptions, like the homily and the universal prayer—are written down and are the same the world over. Not only the words of liturgy, but most of the actions are the same everywhere: standing, sitting, and kneeling. The liturgical books include many rubrics (from the Latin word for "red," because these instructions are sometimes printed in red ink), which give instructions for how and where each part of the liturgy happens. All of this should remind us that the liturgy does not belong to any one person, priest, or parish. The liturgy is the Church's prayer. But, that does not mean that it is not *our* prayer too. In the words of the Second Vatican Council, the liturgy is "the outstanding means whereby the faithful may express in their lives and manifest to others the mystery of Christ and the real nature of the true Church."[9] Liturgy is our means of expression with Christ and about Christ. In other words, liturgy is the language we speak as Catholics.

The liturgy is richly varied. While the liturgy is carefully governed by liturgical books, it is never monotone. It is constantly changing, with different readings for every day of the year, and different prayers for most days. Through the liturgical year, the Church invites us to meditate on different aspects of the mystery of Christ, from his conception to his second coming. The liturgy is colorful!

> The preeminent manifestation of the Church is present in the full, active participation of all God's holy people in these liturgical celebrations, especially in the same eucharist.
>
> —*Sacrosanctum concilium*, 41

The Eucharist is the most important of the Church's liturgies, but it is not our only liturgy. The liturgies of the Church also include rites like those in the *Rite of Christian Initiation of Adults* and the *Order of Christian Funerals*. They include celebrations of the other sacraments, from baptism, confirmation, and Eucharist to anointing and penance, matrimony, and holy orders. In addition, the Liturgy of the Hours, prayed daily by deacons, priests, bishops, religious, and many laypeople, is part of the Church's liturgy, sanctifying the hours of each day with prayer to God.

Liturgy is different from devotion. The Church has a rich and wonderful array of devotional prayer—novenas, chaplets, the Rosary, the Way of the Cross, among others—which can enrich our prayer and bring us closer to Christ and to his Mother. The Rosary has a special place in the life of the Church, for, in the words of St. John Paul II, it "serves as an excellent introduction and

---

9. *Sacrosanctum concilium*, 2. This document is also commonly referred to by its English title, the Constitution on the Sacred Liturgy. The paragraphs in Church documents are numbered sequentially. The references throughout this resource refer to the corresponding paragraph numbers in the quoted document. Universal Church documents are usually issued first in Latin. Throughout this resource, the Latin titles of these documents have been used. The English titles refer to those documents that are issued by the United States Conference of Catholic Bishops. Hereafter, in footnotes this document will be abbreviated as SC.

a faithful echo of the Liturgy, enabling people to participate fully and interiorly in it and to reap its fruits in their daily lives."[10] These devotions can enrich, but must never replace, our participation in the liturgy.

Liturgy both reflects and shapes our faith. A medieval scholar expressed this in a phrase that has become famous: *lex orandi, lex credendi,* which can loosely be translated as "the law of prayer shapes the law of belief." In other words, the way we pray informs our theology. If you look at the footnotes in the documents of the Second Vatican Council, and in the *Catechism of the Catholic Church,* you'll notice that the sources cited for key teachings not only include the Bible and teachings of popes and councils, but prayers from the Mass. Liturgy is a school of prayer and a school of faith, teaching us to believe with the Church.

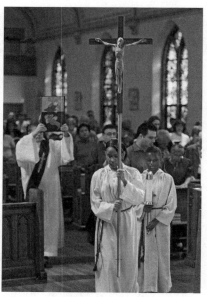

The medieval adage is often extended to read *lex orandi, lex credendi, lex vivendi*— "law of life." The way we pray shapes what we believe—and the way we live our lives. Authentic worship and faith lead to discipleship. If it doesn't, it means the transforming power of the liturgy is not really reaching us. As Pope Benedict XVI has written, "A Eucharist which does not pass over into the concrete practice of love is intrinsically fragmented."[11]

Liturgy really matters. *Sacrosanctum concilium* of the Second Vatican Council had this to say about liturgy: "[T]he liturgy is the summit toward which the activity of the Church is directed; at the same time it is the font from which all Church's power flows."[12] Liturgy is both source and summit, culmination and starting-place. All the preaching and evangelizing the Church

Liturgy is the fountain from which we draw strength to do Christ's work in the world.

does is meant to draw people to Christ in the celebration of the Eucharist. At the same time, though, the Eucharist is not a stopping place. Liturgy is the fountain from which we draw strength to do Christ's work in the world. Liturgy gathers us; liturgy also sends us forth. And if liturgy fails to do that, there is a problem. "We cannot delude ourselves," wrote St. John Paul II, "by our mutual love and, in particular, by our concern for those in need we will be

10. *Rosarium Virginis Mariae,* 4.

11. *Deus caritas est* (DCE), 14.

12. SC, 10.

recognized as true followers of Christ. . . . This will be the criterion by which the authenticity of our Eucharistic celebrations is judged."[13]

The Privilege to Serve

Liturgical ministers have the wonderful privilege of helping others participate in this transforming reality we call the Church's liturgy. Whether we are proclaiming a Scripture reading, taking up the collection, distributing Communion, carrying a candle, or preparing the liturgical environment, our goal is the same: to help others find in the liturgy what we have found—a community of believers, a school of holiness, a place of encounter with Jesus Christ. When we go to Mass, we never come out the same, because liturgy is meant to change us. No wonder, then, that the Church puts such emphasis on participation in the liturgy. If we participate fully, consciously, and actively in the liturgy, we cannot fail to be transformed and do our part to transform the world we live in. As liturgical ministers, we are called to do just that, and to help others do the same.

Questions for Reflection and Discussion

1. How is praying with a community different than praying on your own? Why do you think Jesus calls us to pray in both ways?

2. What liturgies of the Church do you participate in on a regular basis?

3. Where and when do you feel closest to Christ?

4. Think about the ways Christ is present in the liturgy and in the world. Think of a time when you have felt Christ's presence in these places.

5. Do you find that participating in the liturgy affects life outside of the liturgy?

---

13. *Mane nobiscum Domine* (MND), 28.

Chapter Two

The Meaning and History of Your Ministry

Sacred Scripture is of the greatest importance in the celebration of the liturgy.

—*Sacrosanctum concilium, 24*

The Word of God calls us to follow. God speaks to us before we pray or respond. Our relationship does not begin with us speaking to God. It starts when God speaks.

God's Word in the Church and in Our Lives

The Old Testament recounts the story of a chosen people—not of a chosen God. God established a covenant with Abraham, Isaac, and Jacob. God renewed it with Moses and David. The holy men and women of old heard what God wanted and they responded in faith. God chose them. God spoke to them.

Jesus also illustrated this throughout his ministry. He preached in synagogues. He taught the crowds. Dramatically, he called disciples to come and follow him. Occasionally, a Gospel story makes it appear that someone else has made the first move. A rich young man asks if he can become a disciple. A woman approaches Jesus for a cure. But in every case, they have heard Jesus or heard about him. The Holy Spirit has opened their hearts, and they respond to the Word of God.

When you first became a Christian through infant baptism or the catechumenate, you took part in a liturgy about God's call. In the Rite of Acceptance into the Order of Catechumens, the community begins the Mass outside the church or by the door. The celebrant invites the new catechumens inside "to share with us at the table of God's word."[1] He then speaks to them briefly, helping them understand the dignity of God's Word, which is proclaimed and heard in the church. From the first moment catechumens take their place in the assembly of the faithful, they learn that the Bible forms us.

Later on, before they are baptized, the celebrant may conduct a ceremony based on one of the cures from the Gospels. Jesus touched the ears and tongue of a man born unable to hear or speak clearly. In working the miracle, Jesus groaned out the Aramaic word *ephphatha,* which means "be opened."[2] Instantly, the man was healed. He became a paradigm of discipleship. With his ears open and his tongue free, he could hear God's Word and return full

---

1.   *Rite of Christian Initiation of Adults,* (RCIA) 60.
2.   Mark 7:34.

praise. When the celebrant touches the ears and lips of those being baptized, he speaks the same word Jesus did: *ephphatha.* To the evangelists, that unusual word was so powerful that they left it alone. They wrote the Gospels in Greek, but this word appears in its original language. We still use the same Aramaic word today. The celebrant says, "Ephphatha: that is, be opened, that you may profess the faith you hear, to the praise and glory of God."[3]

This ceremony may also be used in the baptism of infants. As they are just beginning to learn the mysteries of human language, we pray that their ears will be opened to God's Word, and that their lips will praise God all their days.[4]

These ceremonies show that our Christian lives begin with and thrive on the Word of God and that we believe that Word has power. Engaging that Word is the privilege and task of every Christian. God's Word called us into discipleship. God's Word guides us throughout discipleship. The more we open our ears, the more the Scripture warms our heart and refreshes our perspective on life.

We hear God's Word in many ways. We spend time with the Bible in private prayer. We refer to it when preparing for special events. We hear preachers and teachers cite specific passages. Most importantly, we hear the Word of God proclaimed at Sunday Mass.

> For it is from Scripture that the readings are given and explained in the homily and that psalms are sung; the prayers, collects, and liturgical songs are scriptural in their inspiration; it is from the Scriptures that actions and signs derive their meaning. Thus to achieve the reform, progress, and adaptation of the liturgy, it is essential to promote that warm and living love for Scripture to which the venerable tradition of both Eastern and Western rites gives testimony.[5]

When we gather with other believers, we form the people of God. Together we have a task to perform: we offer praise to the one who sits on the throne and to the Lamb. While we are there, gathered as one in this sacred place, we open our ears together, so that God might speak to us. Most importantly, it is there at the Eucharist, in the presence of the community of believers, where we hear the Word of God. Listening is one of the ways that we express our unity. One of the duties of the people of God is to form one body, as paragraph 96 of the GIRM explains.

> [The faithful] form one body, whether in hearing the word of God, or in taking part in the prayers and in the singing, or above all by the common offering of Sacrifice and by participating together at the Lord's table.
>
> —*General Instruction of the Roman Missal,* 96

It is easier to seem one body when we perform the same action, assume the same posture, recite the same words, or sing the same songs. But even when it

---

3. RCIA, 199.
4. *Rite of Baptism for Children,* 65.
5. SC, 24.

looks like we are doing nothing—when we are listening—we are one. We are one when we unite our hearts in faith, when we hang onto every word as we do with those we love, when we make ourselves still, rather than miss a single word. When we do this together, we are one.

This is our joy. This is our duty: "The readings from the word of God are to be listened to reverently by everyone, for they are an element of the greatest importance in the Liturgy."[6]

We all have a part to play when we come to Mass. We do not just attend Mass. We participate at Mass. When someone else is speaking, we participate. We listen. We open our ears and prepare our hearts to respond.

Oh yes, to respond. Jesus did not speak casually. God did not invite Abraham and Sarah into the promises of the covenant just to make small talk. God's Word comes to us with a purpose. It demands a response.

"When God communicates his word, he expects a response, one, that is, of listening and adoring 'in Spirit and in truth' (John 4:23). The Holy Spirit makes that response effective, so that what is heard in the celebration of the liturgy may be carried out in a way of life: 'Be doers of the word and not hearers only' (James 1:22)."[7]

Our response, then, is twofold. When God speaks, we respond on the spot by listening and adoring. Then later we carry out the purpose of the Scriptures in our way of life. All that we do is based upon the Word of God. It is our blueprint, our constitution, our mission statement, our compass.

Our response flows naturally when we realize what happens at Mass. God is speaking to us. This is not a mere reading of an ancient document, or a report of something said long ago. It is not lines recited by an actor, or a mere recitation of a letter from someone you know.

God is speaking to us. When the Scriptures are read, it is as if the book disappears. The reader becomes the mouthpiece of God. God uses the voice of the reader to say something modern, something new, something that applies to the world today. Yes, the words are old, but their proclamation is always new. To hear the Scriptures proclaimed is to hear the voice of God speaking right now to the people gathered together for worship.

When the Sacred Scriptures are read in the Church, God himself speaks to his people, and Christ, present in his own word, proclaims the Gospel.

—*General Instruction of the Roman Missal*, 29

The Gospel—more than the other readings—has a very special significance when it is proclaimed. The four Gospels contain the words that Jesus spoke. When a reading from them is proclaimed aloud in the context of the liturgy, Jesus is speaking his words—now, in your church, to you, and to the community. Jesus is speaking.

---

6. GIRM, 29.

7. Introduction, *Lectionary for Mass*, 6.

God has other ways to communicate with us, but this one is favored. God dwells apart from time. The sacred Scriptures, written so long ago, still carry the voice of God today.

The reader has a daunting responsibility. The reader's voice needs to carry God's voice. The reader does not just pronounce words. The reader communicates a divine message.

The Liturgy of the Word within the Mass

The Mass takes place at two "tables"—the table of the Word and the table of the Eucharist. But it is one table. The two parts of the Mass form one profound experience.

"In the Mass is spread the table both of God's Word and of the Body of Christ, and from it the faithful are to be instructed and refreshed."[8]

The furniture is different. The Liturgy of the Word focuses on the ambo. The Liturgy of the Eucharist centers at the altar. These two furnishings draw the attention of the faithful throughout each part of the Mass.

There is one moment at the beginning, however, when the two parts of the Mass may be drawn together. In the entrance procession, the deacon—or in his absence a reader—may carry the *Book of the Gospels* to the sanctuary. Arriving there, the person carrying the book sets it on the altar, makes a reverence, and withdraws. This action does not take place with the lectionary.

The *Book of the Gospels*, true to its name, is the collection of Gospel passages to be read throughout the year. That book may appear on Sundays or other major occasions throughout the year. It may be used for proclamation at any Mass. Having the Gospels in a separate book sets them apart from the other Scriptures. The Gospels are special to us. When it is time to proclaim one at the Eucharist, the liturgy explodes with a variety of symbols. The

The people are fed both from the table of God's Word (ambo) and the Body of Christ (altar).

people stand. The cantor begins the Gospel acclamation. If there is a deacon, he asks the priest for a blessing. If the priest reads the Gospel, he bows to the altar and prays humbly. A procession forms. Candles, incense, and other signs of honor may be carried. A special book is used. The deacon or priest greets the people. The people respond. All trace the sign of the cross on their

---

8. GIRM, 28.

forehead, lips, and heart. The book may be incensed. And then, after all of that, after doing everything we can to draw attention to this book, we hear the words of Jesus.

The *Book of the Gospels* represents Christ. The altar, where the Liturgy of the Eucharist will be celebrated, also represents Christ. So at the beginning of Mass, these two symbols of Christ are brought together in a simple, yet meaningful gesture. The *Book of the Gospels*, carried up to the sanctuary in the entrance procession, is placed on the altar. The words of Jesus are set on the altar of Jesus. The Liturgy of the Word and the Liturgy of the Eucharist are joined as one.

Pope Benedict XVI, in his post-synodal apostolic exhortation *The Word of the Lord* (*Verbum Domini*), has written about the sacramentality of the Word—the way that God is present in the Word and gives it power: "The Word of God can be perceived by faith through the 'sign' of human words and actions. Faith acknowledges God's Word by accepting the words and actions by which he makes himself known to us. . . . The sacramentality of the word can thus be understood by analogy with the real presence of Christ under the appearances of the consecrated bread and wine."[9] Benedict goes on to quote a passage from St. Jerome.

> We are reading the Sacred Scriptures. For me, the Gospel is the Body of Christ; for me, the holy Scriptures are his teaching. And when he says: *Whoever does not eat my flesh and drink my blood* (John 6:53), even though these words can also be understood of the [Eucharistic] Mystery, Christ's body and blood are really the word of Scripture, God's teaching. When we approach the [Eucharistic] Mystery, if a crumb falls to the ground we are troubled. Yet when we are listening to the word of God, and God's Word and Christ's flesh and blood are being poured into our ears yet we pay no heed, what great peril should we not feel?[10]

The Word of God deserves our respect. Readers are not to change the texts of the introduction or conclusion of the reading, nor of the reading itself. The reading was prepared by translators who worked hard to make the original language understandable when read aloud today. The translation has been approved by our bishops and confirmed by the Vatican for proclamation at the liturgy. The opening and closing formulas serve the people, and they do not change. There is no need to introduce the opening formula with another formula, such as "The first reading is a reading from . . . " Just announce, "A reading from . . . " The people more easily open their ears to the reading when they hear the appropriate cue.

---

9. Paragraph 56, in which he refers to SC, 7 that describes the four ways Christ is present in the Mass.
10. Jerome, *In Psalmum*, 147: CCL, 78, 337–338, quoted in Benedict XVI, *The Word of the Lord*, 56.

Indeed, the words take on a deep significance when they are repeated. The repetition of the words from church to church across the world, and from age to age throughout time, indicates their sanctity. The formulas have many layers of meaning that can be plumbed when they are used in the simplest of forms.

The reading closes when the reader says, "The word of the Lord." Some years ago, the reader concluded the reading with "This is the word of the Lord." But the conclusion was changed for various reasons. For example, the Latin text, on which the English translations of the Mass are based, has always had the reader say, "Verbum Domini"; literally, "The word of the Lord."

The initial English translation made sense: "This is the word of the Lord." It made a simple declarative statement about the Word that had been read. But in time, the meaning became obscured. Some readers picked up the book before they announced, "This is the word of the Lord," as if the Word were the book. It is not. The book is special, and it deserves to be handled with reverence because of its sacred contents and purpose. But the Word is not the book. The Word is the spoken Word.

God's Word is alive, spoken through the reader.

To many people, this seemed like a small point, but it aims for a bigger meaning: God still speaks to us. God's Word is not history. It is alive. The liturgy accents this reality.

The practice of distributing copies of the readings so everyone can read along may seem helpful, but actually it confuses the meaning behind the proclamation of Scripture. The Word of God does not dwell in communal *reading*, but in communal *hearing*. When the reader is well prepared, the people are listening and looking at the lector, and the book is less important than the voice, then the reader's words at the end of the reading have an earthshaking meaning: "The word of the Lord." We have just heard God speak to us.[11]

The reading of sacred Scripture has always been an important part of Christian worship. As we know from Jesus' own behavior, it was customary for readings to be proclaimed at the Jewish synagogue. Those early Christians who came from Judaism logically based their worship on ceremonial forms with which they were familiar. That included a reading.

St. Paul asked those who received his letters to read them to other believers. At the end of the First Letter to the Thessalonians, he commands the recipients

11. Those who have a hearing impairment may benefit from a personal copy of the printed text or from a live interpreter.

to read the letter to the entire community.[12] The letter to the Colossians says, "And when this letter is read before you, have it read also in the church of the Laodiceans, and you yourselves read the one from Laodicea."[13] To the Corinthians, he writes, "For we write you nothing but what you can read and understand, and I hope that you will understand completely."[14]

The History of Readers

The proclamation of Scriptures at the Eucharist dates back at least as far as the time of St. Justin. Writing around the year 150, he described a typical gathering of Christians: "The memoirs of the apostles and the writings of the prophets are read, as much as time permits. When the reader has finished, . . ."[15] From this brief witness we recognize the customs of having regular readings and a reader to proclaim them.

It did not take long before some ceremony with the reader began to evolve. In some places in the third or fourth century, a ritual action was taking place before the reading began. The bishop picked up the book and handed it to the reader.[16] In this brief gesture the bishop indicated the worthiness of the book and his appointment of the reader to serve as a minister for the people.

From texts such as these it is clear that a lectionary was used for Christian worship very early on, but no copies of such books have survived. The earliest one comes from the sixth century, and it was not as comprehensive as ours are today. Lectionaries continued to develop throughout the Middle Ages, and the one-year cycle of readings established after the Council of Trent served the Church for four hundred years.

At about the same time, the ministry of reader changed from being a function of the laity to the responsibility of the ordained. Lay ministers proclaimed the Scriptures from the earliest days of the Church, but eventually the title of lector became ceremonial and the task was absorbed into the duties of ordained ministers serving at the altar.

Before a man was ordained to the major order of priesthood, he passed through a series of rituals called minor orders. Originally, the minor orders appointed ministers to perform certain tasks, but in time they evolved into steps toward ordination to the priesthood. One of these made him a lector, but he was a lector more in name than in deed. There were some circumstances when a lector chanted a reading, but normally this function was reserved to a minister of higher rank, the subdeacon.[17]

---

12. See 1 Thessalonians 5:27.
13. See Colossians 4:16.
14. See 2 Corinthians 1:13.
15. *Apology* 1:67. See *Catechism of the Catholic Church,* 1345.
16. *Apostolic Tradition,* 11.
17. After receiving the minor orders, a candidate was ordained to the major orders of subdeacon, deacon, and priest. These ministers vested for Mass and performed assigned functions. The subdiaconate was

The Church made some changes to the ministry of lector after the Second Vatican Council. Pope Paul VI abolished the minor order of lector, a status attained when a bishop ordained a cleric to this function in a liturgical ceremony. But Paul VI retained the title lector as an "instituted" lay ministry, a status still attained in a liturgical ceremony over which the ordinary usually presides. Today's candidates for ordination are installed as "instituted" lectors before they can be ordained deacons or priests. But lectors are no longer considered clerics. The ministry has been returned to the laity, who exercised it at the beginning of Church history. "The function of proclaiming the readings is by tradition not presidential but ministerial."[18]

A person no longer has to be in preparation for priesthood to be instituted as a lector. Paul VI, however, kept the requirement that only lay *men* could be instituted as lectors. He permitted women and non-instituted men to read at Mass, but he did not allow women to be formally instituted in the ministry by the ordinary. In 2021, however, Pope Francis changed the Code of Canon Law, giving women access to the instituted ministries of lector and acolyte, and he recognized that these ministries are now understood to be rooted in baptism rather than ordination.[19]

Consequently, very few dioceses have *instituted* lectors serving in parishes. Men and women share this ministry equally as *non-instituted, commissioned* readers. They may obtain a certificate of service if that is the local custom, but they are not formally installed into the ministry by the ordinary.

The *General Instruction of the Roman Missal* (GIRM) still makes some references to instituted lectors. For example, it expects instituted lectors to be vested (336) and seated in the sanctuary (195). (GIRM 339 says that lay ministers wear "appropriate or dignified clothing," and this could apply to instituted lectors as well.) But the GIRM does permit other commissioned lay people to proclaim the readings at Mass: "In the absence of an instituted lector, other lay people may be deputed to proclaim the readings from Sacred Scripture, people who are truly suited to carry out this function and carefully prepared."[20] The Church has been blessed by their service.

The Reader's Role during Mass and Its Significance

The reader's role takes place during the Liturgy of the Word. The main parts of this first half of the Mass are the readings from sacred Scripture and the

---

eliminated after the Second Vatican Council.
18. GIRM, 59.
19. The Apostolic Letter, *Spiritus Domini*, was promulgated on January 10, 2021. It modified canon 230, paragraph 1: "Lay persons who possess the age and qualifications established by decree of the conference of bishops can be admitted on a stable basis through the prescribed liturgical rite to the ministries of lector and acolyte."
20. GIRM, 101.

music occurring between them. Periods of silence, the homily, the creed, and the prayer of the faithful fill out the Liturgy of the Word.

Because of the great responsibility of minsters of the Word, they need a multifaceted training:

> Their preparation must above all be spiritual, but what may be called a technical preparation is also needed. The spiritual preparation presupposes at least a biblical and liturgical formation. The purpose of their biblical formation is to give readers the ability to understand the readings in context and to perceive by the light of faith the central point of the revealed message. The liturgical formation ought to equip the readers to have some grasp of the meaning and structure of the Liturgy of the Word and of the significance of its connection with the Liturgy of the Eucharist. The technical preparation should make the readers more skilled in the art of reading publicly, either with the power of their own voice or with the help of sound equipment.[21]

Readers may serve on other occasions besides Mass, but they should be most familiar with their responsibilities at the Eucharist.

Readers have the following duties. They join the entrance procession of the Mass, and they may carry the *Book of the Gospels* if there is no deacon present. Readers proclaim the readings that precede the Gospel. They observe silences after each reading. If there is no one to sing the psalm, a reader may lead the refrain and proclaim the verses; however, it is preferable that the psalm be sung.[22]

If the deacon does not lead the prayer of the faithful, a reader may do so. If no one sings the entrance and communion antiphons of the Mass, and if the people do not recite them, the reader may read them.[23]

The reader's role concludes with the Liturgy of the Word. The reader continues, however, to participate fully at Mass throughout the Liturgy of the Eucharist. By custom, the reader does not walk out at the end of Mass in procession with the other ministers.[24] The reader leaves as a member of the faithful, all of whom are sent forth into the world to bring the Word of God to all they meet.

The reader's services take up only a few minutes at Mass, but these are critical minutes. Even when processing to the altar at the beginning of Mass or to the ambo before the reading, the reader carries a sense of purpose. People will begin to comprehend the significance of the reading by the seriousness with which the reader approaches this task.

---

21. Introduction, *Lectionary for Mass*, 55.

22. GIRM, 61.

23. GIRM, 194–198.

24. See page 61, note 3, in this resource. A lector who has been instituted, is vested in the garb proper to the ministerial role, and has been sitting in the sanctuary for Mass, would walk out with other ministers at the end. However, the *Book of the Gospels* is not processed out at the end of Mass. Be familiar with the customs of your parish and diocese.

In the proclamation of the Word, the people will realize how well the reader understands the reading. The reader's preparation will be evident by the way the reading sounds. The preparation is more than technical, grammatical, and mental. It is, above all, spiritual.

You have offered to serve your community as a reader. You have reflected on the gifts God gave you: a love for the Bible, an understanding of God's Word, an ability to communicate, the willingness to proclaim the Scripture in a public place, a love for the liturgy of the Church, and an appreciation of its calendar of feasts and seasons.

You will exercise a variety of functions: proclaiming the Word, leading the psalm (if a cantor is not present), and offering the prayer of the faithful. You will need to grasp why these words are important each week—what it is that God is saying to the Church, and how the petitions express the hopes and desires of the local community.

> In the readings, as explained by the Homily, God speaks to his people, opening up to them the mystery of redemption and salvation and offering spiritual nourishment, and Christ himself is present through his word in the midst of the faithful.
>
> —*General Instruction of the Roman Missal*, 55

You will also be called upon to manage silences. Before you begin to read, you will want to have the attention of the entire assembly. After each reading you will pause and pray, modeling the reflection that all will do. Even the way you pace the petitions during the prayer of the faithful will help people think about them one by one. They will think about what circumstances need prayer this week and why these petitions have surfaced. Your recitation of these intentions will make it clear that you are anxious to pray them, inviting others to do so as well.

In order to "more fittingly and perfectly fulfill these functions," Paul VI recommends this profoundly direct expectation of a reader: you are "to meditate assiduously on the sacred Scripture."[25]

Questions for Reflection and Discussion

1. What was your experience with Scripture when you were younger, and how has your relationship with it changed over the years?

2. Name a time when a passage from the Bible particularly moved you.

3. Who are some readers who have served as models for you? How did they read? How did they live?

4. During the Liturgy of the Word at Mass, what do you do as a member of the assembly? What could you do?

---

25. Apostolic Letter issued *Motu Proprio*, by which the Discipline of First Tonsure, Minor Orders, and Subdiaconate in the Latin Church is Reformed, in *The Installation of Readers and Acolytes, Admission to Candidacy for Ordination as Deacons and Priests*.

Chapter Three

Serving as a Reader

Ezra read plainly from the book of the law of God, interpreting it so that
all could understand what was read. Then . . . [he] said to all the people:
"Today is holy to the LORD your God. Do not be sad, and do not weep"—
for all the people were weeping as they heard the words of the law.

—Nehemiah 8:8–10

Having been deprived of the Word of God during the many years of the exile, the people to whom Ezra proclaimed the Word were overcome with emotion—a very different response from today's assemblies. Fed regularly on the readings as we are, perhaps we become complacent. Could the proclamation of God's Word, when thoughtfully prepared and delivered with understanding and expression, help draw people into the text and touch their hearts? The people's response to Ezra's reading might well prompt readers of today to reflect on their responsibility for proclaiming the Word of God to their own assemblies.

Overview of the Role of the Reader

The Church intends that readers should be "truly suited to carrying out this function and carefully prepared, so that by their hearing the readings from the sacred texts the faithful may conceive in their hearts a sweet and living affection for Sacred Scripture."[1] Has the heartfelt, prepared, and practiced proclamation of the readings at Mass led you to a sweet and living affection for Scripture? Has it pulled you into the text and opened you to its meanings?

Now that you are preparing to be a reader, it falls to you to bring this power of the Word of God and love of Scripture to others. If this sounds daunting, remember that you have been called to this ministry by the Holy Spirit. Perhaps on the surface you answered a request from your community. Perhaps you felt (either spontaneously or gradually) your own desire to enter into the ministry. Nevertheless, on a deeper level the Spirit has been working and will continue to work in you to help you discern your role. Throughout your training and your practice of the ministry, stay open to further promptings from within that help you consider if this is a good fit, if it feels "right," and if you can feel your own love of Scripture growing.

Some nervousness may always be natural, and a healthy sense of humility in the face of what you are doing is appropriate. But remember also that you are already skilled and blessed, and that the community is grateful you will share your gifts. Through resources such as this book and training sessions at

---

1. *General Instruction on the Roman Missal*, 101.

Understanding what you proclaim depends on knowing the Bible.

your parish, you are receiving the careful preparation that will allow you to lead others to the love of Scripture that you already possess.

The good effect of your ministry begins with and always depends upon this: that you yourself understand what you're reading. As a minister of the Word, you are continually pressing deeper into the mysteries that these texts offer. Only by praying and studying a text can you proclaim it with understanding and conviction. What contributes to an effective proclamation? Aside from the basics (speaking clearly and loudly enough to be heard), the assembly needs to feel, by the expressive way you proclaim, that you understand what you are reading—and that you believe it. You would like your hearers to come away from your reading with a sense of the depth and power of these texts conveyed by one who knows their author.

The Bible—the Great Book behind the Lectionary

The readings we hear at Mass are proclaimed from the lectionary—a collection of Scripture passages taken from the Bible and arranged in the order of the liturgical year. The *Lectionary for Mass* will be discussed in pages to come, but first it's important to know that the designers of the lectionary presume that the faithful—and especially proclaimers—know something about the stories and characters and circumstances of the Bible from which the readings are taken. The Church expects that in addition to hearing Scripture proclaimed at Mass, Catholics are reading the Bible on their own.

Why is reading and studying the Bible so crucial? Why are the words of the Bible interwoven throughout the prayers and readings and songs of the Mass? As Paul Turner explained in chapter 1, it is one of the primary ways we receive the Word of God. Sacred Scripture is a sacramental word that mirrors Jesus' presence in the Eucharist:

> The Church has always venerated the divine scriptures as she venerated the Body of the Lord, in so far as she never ceases, particularly in the sacred liturgy, to partake of the bread of life and to offer it to the faithful from the one table of the Word of God and the Body of Christ.[2]

Behind the Scripture readings you will proclaim at the ambo stands the Bible from which they come.

Know the Basic Parts and Books of the Bible

Before diving into this book of God's Word, let's step back to see the big picture of its contents. The Bible is a collection of texts written in different literary styles in different eras, and even expressing different perspectives. Most of the Old Testament books were written in Hebrew, a few in Aramaic. All of the New Testament books were written in Greek. Some Old Testament books of the Bible depend on earlier oral traditions that in turn were probably written between 1000 BC and the century before Christ. All of the books of the New Testament were written in the second half of the first century AD. Despite the diversity of these texts, they nevertheless form an organic whole— telling the long story of God's love for his people.

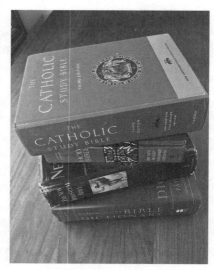

The major categories in the Christian Bible are Old Testament and New Testament. (What we Christians call "the Old Testament" is for Jews "The Hebrew Bible." Jews and Christians both read and venerate these ancient sacred texts, although we interpret and even arrange them differently.)

Using a Catholic study Bible is a good way to learn about the Bible. It's also helpful to consult various versions of the Bible and use Bible reference works.

---

2. *Dei Verbum (Dogmatic Constitution on Divine Revelation)*, 21.

Old Testament

Pentateuch
 Genesis
 Exodus
 Leviticus
 Numbers
 Deuteronomy
Historical Books
 Joshua
 Judges
 Ruth
 1 and 2 Samuel
 1 and 2 Kings
 1 and 2 Chronicles
 Ezra
 Nehemiah
Biblical Novellas
 Tobit
 Judith
 Esther
 1 and 2 Maccabees
Wisdom Books
 Job
 Psalms
 Proverbs
 Ecclesiastes
 Song of Songs
 Wisdom
 Sirach
Prophetic Books
 Isaiah
 Jeremiah
 Lamentations
 Baruch
 Ezekiel
 Daniel
 Hosea
 Joel
 Amos
 Obadiah

 Jonah
 Micah
 Nahum
 Habakkuk
 Zephaniah
 Haggai
 Zechariah
 Malachi

New Testament

Gospels and Acts
 Matthew
 Mark
 Luke
 John
 Acts of the Apostles
Letters of Paul
 Romans
 1 and 2 Corinthians
 Galatians
 Philippians
 1 Thessalonians
 Philemon
Letters Traditionally Ascribed to Paul
 Ephesians
 Colossians
 2 Thessalonians
 1 and 2 Timothy
 Titus
 Philemon
 Hebrews
General Letters and Revelation
 James
 1 and 2 Peter
 1, 2, and 3 John
 Jude
 Revelation to John

The first five books of the Bible are called the Pentateuch, and they tell the most foundational stories of Israel's faith for both Jews and Christians. The Book of Genesis tells of the creation, the promise and establishment of the covenant, the land, and the chosen people—all through stories of our earliest ancestors in faith.

From Exodus comes the crucial narrative of Moses leading the people out of Egypt, across the Red Sea on dry land, and through the wilderness for forty years. It tells of God establishing a covenant with them with the Ten Commandments as its cornerstone. The Book of Leviticus records the detailed laws for the ritual life and holiness of the priests and people. Numbers retells the story of the desert years, and Deuteronomy looks back yet again to the exodus and wandering, but from the perspective of the laws of the covenant as the people stand on the brink of entering the Promised Land.

The historical books tell the story of the people of Israel from the time they reach the Promised Land through the periods of the judges and the establishment of the monarchy with King Saul, then the stories of King David, Solomon, and the kings that followed, the two kingdoms of Israel and Judah, the harrowing stories of the conquest of both kingdoms, the exile to Babylon, and finally the Israelites' return home to resettle the land and rebuild their lives.

Several books are stories set in particular historical situations that are intended to teach people about God's ways and to encourage them in times of crisis, such as the story of Ruth, the Moabite woman who gives herself completely to her adopted Israelite family and to Israel's God—with happy results. Another story is about Esther, the Jewish queen of a Persian ruler, who, with her uncle, Mordecai, is able to thwart the plan of the king's chief officer to have all Jews slaughtered.

The wisdom books teach how to act wisely in everyday life—sometimes in very practical ways but sometimes, as in the Books of Job and Ecclesiastes, they refer to deeper questions such as why people experience suffering. The Book of Proverbs personifies wisdom as a woman who was God's companion at creation. Wisdom is presented as a quality or gift that all should try to attain. Also included in this category is the Book of Psalms, the collection of prayers that were sung in the temple and presented as models of prayer for God's people of all times.

The books of the prophets bring us teachings and exhortations that convey the threat of judgment and promise of salvation from various times in Israel's history. Prophets such as Isaiah, Jeremiah, and Ezekiel speak to the people for God in particular situations, but in poetic ways that are meaningful for believers of all times.

The New Testament contains the sacred texts written by the early Christian community.

In the Gospel accounts Christians find their most sacred texts, presenting the culmination of the great story of salvation—of God's self-revelation. The four accounts came from four different sources that tradition ascribes to individuals named Matthew, Mark, Luke, and John, although in many ways they are accounts produced by communities rather than by individuals. Each tells the story of Christ's life, death, and resurrection from a different perspective, each revealing its own insights about our Lord. Matthew, Mark, and Luke all seem to use similar sources and cover many of the same details. For that reason they are called the "synoptic" Gospels (*syn* meaning "together" and *optic* meaning "to see"; so "seeing together" because of their similar perspective). John differs from the other three by including some stories that do not appear in them. It also focuses on the spiritual meaning behind Jesus' words and on Jesus' strong identification with the Father ("The Father and I are one" [John 10:30]).

The Acts of the Apostles was written as the second volume of the Gospel according to Luke by the same author. It reports the activities of the apostles as they follow Christ's command to "make disciples of all nations" throughout the Mediterranean world. Beginning with the ascension of the Lord and focusing on the leadership of Peter and Paul, it includes the account of the Church's early crucial turn to incorporate the Gentiles and ends with Paul's first imprisonment in Rome.

The fourteen letters in this section of the New Testament have been attributed to Paul according to tradition. Hebrews, however, is not actually in the form of a letter and does not claim to be by Paul, so it has long been understood to be a later treatise written in Paul's style. Many scholars now agree that Ephesians, Colossians, Second Thessalonians, and First and Second Timothy were written by Paul's disciples, leaving Romans, First and Second Corinthians, Galatians, Philippians, First Thessalonians, and Philemon as genuine letters of Paul.

Paul's writings are earlier than any of the Gospel accounts. Those written in his name by disciples are either from around the same time as the Gospels or somewhat later. All of these letters, in various ways, unfold the mystery of Christ for the contemplation of his followers and show Christians how to live their human lives on a new plane in imitation of Christ.

The letters often referred to as the "catholic" or "universal" letters seem not to address particular communities, but are intended for a wider audience. Like the other letters, they discuss the practical implications of living in community as Christians.

The last book of the New Testament describes an awe-filled vision about events in the future culmination of history. It is written in a style called "apocalyptic"—a type of writing that is dramatic and visionary. It was intended to give hope to Christians in very perilous times, to help them endure hardships with faith, by revealing that there would be justice and fulfillment in the end.

Know the Stories of Salvation History

Our knowledge of Scripture grows out of a sense for the whole story, the characters who populate them, and how all these books fit together. Effective proclaimers want to learn the grand arc of the story of salvation—from the beginnings, to humanity's first understandings of God, to the prophecies about God's plan, to its fulfillment in Jesus Christ, to the proclamation of Christ in the new Christian community, and finally, to the anticipation of the revelation of God's kingdom.

The lectionary is designed to tell this story in bits and pieces during the course of the liturgical year. You'll notice that the stories of the Lord's two comings are told during Advent—both the waiting and longing of people for the coming of the Messiah and the anticipation of Christ's second coming at the end of time. During Christmas Time we hear the wondrous stories around the birth of Jesus and we meditate on what this arrival of God in human form will mean for us. The Feast of the Baptism of the Lord at the end of Christmas Time inaugurates Jesus' ministry so that we hear about the calling of the disciples and the early stories of Jesus' ministry during Ordinary Time in the winter.

During Lent especially we hear the retelling of salvation history: stories of temptation, sin, mercy, sacrifice, and redemption, including the three great Gospel stories from John, intended to instruct the elect, as well as the entire assembly, about the movement from darkness to light and from death to life through Jesus Christ. Palm Sunday, Holy Thursday, and Good Friday tell us of the days leading up to and including the passion and crucifixion. At the great Easter Vigil, as we await the resurrection, we hear again highlights of the history of God's relationship to humanity, culminating with the rising of Christ from death and the significance of the baptisms that will be performed on this night.

During Easter Time we ponder the significance of the paschal mystery and follow the key events in the life of the new Christian community. We hear how Paul develops his teaching. Then, on Pentecost, we hear the narratives of the coming of the Holy Spirit. During the long summer and autumn period of Ordinary Time we attend to Jesus' teachings on discipleship—how we should live. Finally, as we approach the end of the year in autumn, we begin to hear more about the end of time.

Throughout the liturgical year, we hear tantalizing excerpts from the major stories that mark God's saving relationship with humanity. As you grow in your knowledge of the Bible, you will want to dive more deeply into these stories in their original contexts—either by reading them on your own or joining Bible study groups.

Creation (Genesis 1—2)

Fall (Genesis 3)

Covenant with Noah (Genesis 6:5—9:17)

Abraham and Sarah (Genesis 11:27—25:11)

Isaac and Rebekah (Genesis 21—35)

Jacob, Rachel, and Leah (Genesis 25:19—50)

Joseph (Genesis 37—50)

The Exodus (Exodus 1—15:21)

Giving of the Ten Commandments (Exodus 18:28—44)

David (1 Samuel 16—1 Kings 2; 1 Chronicles 2—29)

The Prophets, Exile, and Restoration (Amos, Isaiah, Jeremiah, Ezekiel)
     (2 Chronicles, Ezra, Nehemiah)

Infancy Narratives of Jesus (Matthew 1—2; Luke 1:3—2)

Temptation of Jesus (Matthew 4:1—11; Mark 1:12—13; Luke 4:1—13)

Baptism of Jesus (Matthew 3:13—17; Mark 1:9—11; Luke 3:21—22)

Calling and Training of Disciples (Matthew 4:18—22; Mark 1:16—20;
     Luke; John 1:35—51)

Teaching and Healing Mission of the Kingdom of God (throughout the
     four Gospels)

Gradual Revelation of Jesus' Identity as Son of God (throughout the four
     Gospels but especially in John)

Passion; Crucifixion; Resurrection; Ascension (Matthew 26—28;
     Mark 14—16; Luke 22—24; John 18—21; Ascension in Acts 1:6—12)

Coming of the Holy Spirit at Pentecost (Acts 2:1—13)

Develop a Grasp of the Time Line

Another way of creating a scaffold for your understanding of the Bible is to
have a general grasp of the sequence of events.

Time Line of Major Turning Points of Biblical Salvation History

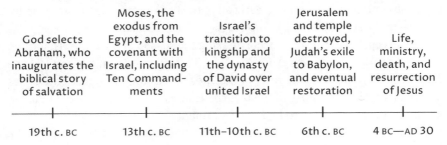

God selects Abraham, who inaugurates the biblical story of salvation	Moses, the exodus from Egypt, and the covenant with Israel, including Ten Commandments	Israel's transition to kingship and the dynasty of David over united Israel	Jerusalem and temple destroyed, Judah's exile to Babylon, and eventual restoration	Life, ministry, death, and resurrection of Jesus
19th c. BC	13th c. BC	11th–10th c. BC	6th c. BC	4 BC—AD 30

Translations and Versions of the Bible

Because these texts were originally written in ancient languages, most of us
know them only through translations into our vernacular languages. A

Catholic study Bible will have extensive and helpful notes about word meanings (as well as other useful information). The Catholic *Lectionary for Mass* follows the New American Bible Revised Edition, and while that is the most commonly used Catholic version of the Bible, other translations are approved by the Church for prayer and study. When preparing to proclaim a text, readers may want to consult these editions, especially the New Revised Standard Version and the New Jerusalem Bible.

Throughout its history, the Church has studied and meditated deeply on the whole Bible. From it, Catholic biblical and liturgical scholars selected some of the most potent and fruitful portions to be set within the revolving wheel of the liturgical year in our lectionary. There the Scripture excerpts take on additional power and meaning from the season or feast we are celebrating as we hear them. Catholics can appreciate those texts even more, however, and readers can proclaim them more effectively when they also know them from their original context in the Bible.

The Lectionary

Our lectionary, in its current form, is a gift of the Second Vatican Council. The one-year Sunday lectionary from before the council expanded into a three-year cycle of readings: years A, B, and C. During Ordinary Time, each year features one Gospel: Matthew, Mark, and Luke, respectively. The Gospel according to John appears during the Easter season all three years, as well as on other occasions such as the Second Sunday in Ordinary Time each year, many of the Sundays of Lent, and some of the summer Sundays of year B.

On the Sundays of Ordinary Time, the first reading comes from somewhere in the Old Testament. It always bears a thematic relationship to the Gospel. During other times of the year, the first reading explores a theme relating to the season. For example, the first readings of Lent tell a sequence of stories from salvation history, leading up to the promise of our redemption. Over the course of three years, nearly all of the books of the Old Testament are represented in the Sunday lectionary.

An exception to this plan occurs during the season of Easter. At that time, the first reading is drawn from the New Testament—from the Acts of the Apostles. There we hear the story of the apostolic Church as it faced struggles and rejoiced in the promise of the resurrection. For the seven weeks of Easter, all the readings come from the New Testament.

The responsorial psalm is chosen because it relates to a theme from the first reading. There are a few exceptions when the psalm pertains more to the season of the year or even to the Gospel. It is permissible to substitute another psalm that fits the occasion, especially if the parish has a musical setting of it in its repertoire.[3]

---

3. GIRM, 61.

The second readings during Ordinary Time are semicontinuous excerpts of different New Testament books. For example, each year Ordinary Time begins with a series of readings from Paul's First Letter to the Corinthians. Although large parts of the letter are never read, the passages we hear follow the thought of the letter from beginning to end over the entire three-year cycle. During the other times of the year, the second reading is chosen because it relates to the feast or season being celebrated. For example, the second readings of Advent show how the early Christians expected Christ would come again very soon, and how they challenged one another to live accordingly.

The Lectionary and the Liturgical Year

As we've seen, all of the readings we hear on a Sunday have been chosen to fit together in a particular way—the images, stories, and meanings intertwine with each other and with the particular moment in the liturgical year to provide food for our lives. Exactly how this happens each Sunday is a fascinating design to figure out each week as you prepare to proclaim your assigned reading. A careful and prayerful reading of those Scriptures during the week leading up to Sunday will open you to the meanings in your reading and to the many ways in which the all the readings of the day are intimately connected to the entire liturgical celebration—its prayers, music, and movements.

It is also helpful to read through the cycle of readings for an entire season, especially Advent, Christmas, Lent, and Easter. That broad overview will help you appreciate your reading in the context of the development of meanings throughout the whole season as well as on its particular Sunday. Each Mass leads us through the mystery of Christ's passion, death, and resurrection. Each liturgical season does the same in an even broader context, focusing us on preparing for God's living presence in our lives here and now, celebrating the fullness of joy at the Word of God alive in our midst, calling us back to our Lord when we have fallen away, and leading us to marvel at the tomb still empty and resplendent in the glory of resurrection and never-ending life. Reading through a long stretch of Ordinary Time gives us a greater and deeper appreciation of the mystery of God in our own lives and in the lives of our communities and the world. The chart on page 26 will give you an overview of the main recurring themes of the liturgical seasons and Ordinary Time.

The repetition of seasons and readings over the years should not tempt us to be complacent in our preparation. Each time we approach our ministry we try to be open to where God is calling us now. We can probably each remember hearing these beginning words of the Gospel: "In those days a decree went out from Caesar Augustus that the whole world should be enrolled,"[4] and by the name *Augustus* we knew the rest of the reading and were consequently

---

4. Luke 2:1.

looking at the poinsettias in the sanctuary, gazing at the stained glass windows, and thinking about our crèche scene at home. We might have heard a reading year after year, one that we know so well that we have it labeled in our minds ("The Three Magi," "The Prodigal Son"). But our challenge as readers in our preparation and in our participation at each Mass is to be truly open to hearing the entire reading and its call to us here and now.

Liturgical Season	Primary Theme or Focus*
Advent	**Celebrating Christ's Two Comings** · First two weeks · The second coming of Christ reigning over all creation in glory · Longing and waiting for the return of the Lord · Second two weeks · Preparing to celebrate · the incarnation · Recalling the birth of Christ
Christmas Time	**Celebrating the Incarnation** · Wedding of heaven and earth · Manifestation of God in Jesus Christ in the incarnation · Light in the darkness · Coming of the reign of God
Ordinary Time in Winter	**Christ's Identity and Ministry; Our Discipleship** · Beginning of Christ's public life and ministry · Calling of the disciples · Christ's teachings for disciples
Lent	**Preparing to Renew Our Baptism** · Recommitting to our faith · Deepening our conversion to Christ and the Gospel · Journeying with the elect as they prepare for their baptism
Sacred Paschal Triduum	**Commemorating the Passion, Death, and Resurrection of Christ**
Easter Time	**Reflecting on and Living the Paschal Mystery** · Mystagogy on the Easter sacraments · The risen Christ among us · New and eternal life · New and eternal life · Living no longer for ourselves
Ordinary Time in Summer and Autumn	**Christ's Identity and Ministry; Our Discipleship** · Christ's preaching and teaching · Disciples living their faith · Mission of the Church · Hard teachings · Approach of the end times

This table was composed by D. Todd Williamson.

One of the great joys of our faith is that we can never delve too deeply into mystery. While we may know these readings well, we can hear them differently each time we encounter them. As the years go by, we change and grow and are not quite the same as we were when last this Scripture was proclaimed to us. We can assume the same of the entire assembly gathered: that over time we all change. We face births and deaths in our families, joys and setbacks in our lives, and we continue to encounter God speaking to us through his Word. If we truly listen in our preparation and at Mass, we may hear what we have not heard in a reading before or be called back to something we have heard but need to hear again. We can never allow the repetition of the seasons or the cycle of readings to keep us from recognizing that this time of listening is a fresh and new encounter with our Lord.

There is yet another dimension to the liturgical year our lectionary follows. The Sundays and seasons, the solemnities, feasts, and memorials with their assigned readings evoke our lives beyond this earthly time, our place in God's eternal and cosmic realm. We hear the stories of salvation history and we know God's love for us and the world he created are always drawing us closer, and that our salvation is still unfolding. We ponder the stories of Christ's incarnation, his life, passion, death, resurrection, and ascension; we know that he is with us, that his paschal mystery is working throughout all creation now. We celebrate the saints and remember that they celebrate with us in every time and place. We hear Jesus' commands to his first disciples and go out to fulfill our own baptismal mission. As readers, we lend our voices to these mysteries.

Particularly because readers voice God's own words to his people, we must be well-prepared and careful not to improvise or add any personal touch to our ministry. Readers help the assembly focus on the Word of God, not on ourselves. In our movements, proclamation, and presence as ministers, we do everything with mindful humility so that the assembly can experience the word of God without distraction.

Developing a Process for Preparing a Reading

The willingness of your parish to train you as a reader indicates that you already possess good basic skills on which to build, but you will learn many others to enhance your work as a reader. You will strengthen your skills for studying and interpreting Scripture, you will train your tongue to be nimble and your voice to be expressive, and you will develop ways of praying and reflecting on the Word of God. There is always more to learn about understanding and proclaiming the Scriptures, so we should never let a feeling of accomplishment stop us from trying to do better. A spirit of humility, awe for the Word of God, and a deep sense of responsibility to the community will help us approach this ministry well.

Among the many ways that you can prepare each week for your ministry, it is often helpful to gather with other readers from the parish. Meeting early in the week to discuss the genres and themes of the readings, pray through the Scriptures, and practice your proclamation can give insight and support for the work.

Whether or not you find that opportunity, your individual preparation is essential. Through it you reflect deeply on both the Word of God and the means of proclaiming it. Scripture is not simply another piece of literature. Detailed study and reflection on the reading allow you to move past the mechanics of reading and be truly disposed to the mystery of God's Word. When we awaken to the mystery and meaning of a reading and its proclamation, we can bring that mystery and meaning to the assembly and truly serve our communities well. If we only worry about the mechanics of the reading, we may give an adequate public speaking performance, but it will be difficult to provide people with the depth to which readers aspire.

Start with Prayer.

This is the grounding you need. Thank God for his Word and for all the blessings of your life. Ask God for guidance and wisdom as you work. Ask for insights about how to communicate the Word to the community. Ask God to free you from self-consciousness, self-doubt, pride, and anything else that would block your preparation.

Read the Passage Aloud.

From the outset, voice the reading numerous times to let your mind and your mouth begin to know it. Then turn to studying the text.

Identify Genre, Speaker, Theme, and Voice

Understanding the genre, speaker, and theme of the reading will go a long way toward determining the most effective way to proclaim it. Genres are literary types that have a characteristic style, form, and subject matter. There are several *genres* that occur frequently in the lectionary.

Narrative: A narrative is a story. We often encounter these in the first readings from the Old Testament and the Acts of the Apostles. Think of the stories of the people of Israel crossing the Red Sea, wandering in the desert, and crying out for lack of water. Remember the stories of the first Christian community that we hear during the Easter season. Stories often have descriptions, drama, and dialogue. The proclaimer must decide how to make the story clear and compelling, including differentiating the voices of different characters.

Discourse: A discourse is generally a speech, lecture, or letter that makes an argument or explanation. Discourse can be found in the Gospel readings in the sermons of Jesus. The Sermon on the Mount, or the Sermon

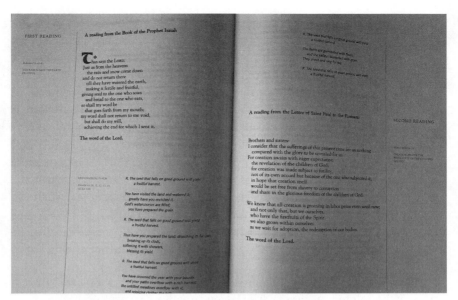

Learn to distinguish different genres or forms of readings: narrative, discourse, poetry, and prayer.

on the Plain, or the five "Bread of Life" readings from the Gospel according to John (during Ordinary Time in the summer in year B) are good examples of discourses. The writings of Paul or the other epistle writers are often discourses. They are addressed to specific communities in order to clarify theology, make arguments for the Christian life, and exhort the audience to live it more fully. They probably respond to questions the writer has received. Readings that are discourses usually have clearly identifiable speakers.

Poetry: Poems can be recognized most often by their layout on the page, but also by their metaphors, repetition, and cadence, as they speak to the deeper truths of God and life. The beautiful creation story from Genesis 1, although presented in paragraph layout, is unmistakably poetic. Poetry can be seen in the sometimes thundering, sometimes comforting proclamations of the prophets, the laments of Job, the versified advice of the wisdom books, and the awe-inspiring visions in the Book of Revelation. Often passages of poetry are found within a narrative, as when Moses and the Israelites sing to the Lord the beautiful hymn in Exodus 15.

Most poetry has a natural flow and meter; often there is repetition or parallel structure in the verses that requires careful preparation so that the assembly can experience its effect and meaning. Some of the most lovely and memorable phrases from Scripture are poetry.

The speaker in a poetic reading is sometimes unnamed, as in the creation story, but can often be identified. Notice how the prophets are careful to signal when they speak in their own voice and when they speak in the voice of God.

Prayer: Much of the prayer in Scripture is poetic and needs a similar approach for proclamation. Prayer in the Bible is much like prayer in our worship or private lives: it takes on many forms and functions but is generally thanksgiving or intercession prayed by humans to God.

Biblical prayer is seen most frequently in the psalms, the prayers Jesus often prayed. If you are asked to proclaim the psalm at a Mass where there is no cantor to lead the assembly in singing it, remember that the psalm is always addressed to God and always proclaimed with great reverence.

Once you have determined the genre and speaker of the reading, consider the *theme or message.* Knowing the theme or point of a narrative, discourse, poem, or prayer will allow you to proclaim effectively. For example, when you prepare the proclamation of a narrative with an understanding of the theme of the story (for example, forgiveness, obedience, betrayal, or restoration), the assembly will hear a cohesive and purposeful reading rather than a list of seemingly random events.

As previously mentioned, the first reading and Gospel reading will almost certainly be related by theme. The second reading may be related, or may relate better to the previous or subsequent week's second reading. It may be part of a semicontinuous reading of an epistle. But recognizing that passage's theme or identifying its central message will help you to give life and meaning to the reading as you proclaim it.

Understanding the speaker and theme of the text will lead you to the *voice* or mood that the text conveys. It is important that the tone and expression of your proclamation be consistent with this speaker and mood and, therefore, with the theme. For example, the voice you use to proclaim the command from God in the book of Joel to "return to me with your whole heart"[5] will have a different tone than the voice you use to proclaim Paul's charge to the Ephesians to "watch carefully how you live,"[6] or the tone you use to proclaim the touching story of the boy Samuel awakening to the presence of God.[7] If you are proclaiming the first reading on the Solemnity of the Epiphany of the Lord, a wooden facial expression and monotone voice make no sense as you proclaim, "Rise up in Splendor, Jerusalem! Your light has come, the glory of the Lord shines upon you."[8] The mood of awe and rejoicing that surrounds all the readings for Epiphany absolutely requires an expressive face and voice conveying wonder and joy.

A good preparation aid for readers, a biblical commentary, or a study Bible can also help you identify the genre and theme of your reading. These resources often explain how Scripture scholars have looked at the text. They give the

---

5. Ash Wednesday, *Lectionary for Mass*, 219.
6. Twentieth Sunday in Ordinary Time, year B, *Lectionary for Mass*, 119.
7. Second Sunday in Ordinary Time, year B, *Lectionary for Mass*, 65.
8. *Lectionary for Mass*, 20.

origins of certain words, describe relevant ancient customs, and provide insights and interpretations that may not be familiar to you. Some of these resources can also be quite dense, so if they are helpful, use them; if not, do not push your preparation to the point of frustration. The resource section beginning on page 62 provides helpful tools for preparation, study, and prayer.

Learn about the Biblical and Historical Context of the Reading

While you are looking at the theme and genre of a reading and gauging its mood, you will also want to look at the overall context of that piece. Find the reading in the Bible to see what comes before and after. The introductions and notes in a good study Bible or biblical commentary will give much helpful background. Questions to ask yourself about the overall context of the reading include:

- Who are the main characters? What are their roles in this reading? Have they appeared elsewhere in the Bible? If so, do they have a backstory that would help you understand this passage?
- What is the setting (time and place) of this reading? For example, are the people in Canaan or are they scattered during the Babylonian exile? Is this taking place in the northern or southern kingdom? Is the community addressed in this reading in ancient Israel or one of Paul's far-flung communities in Turkey or Greece? Does the setting give any additional information about what is going on? (Although some Bibles have maps, an atlas of the Bible can be inexpensive and extremely helpful for looking up physical locations and learning about the lands in the reading.)
- What are the historical events surrounding this reading? For example, is this in the time of the ancestors, or the judges, or the kings? (Study Bibles have detailed time lines in their appendixes that will help you place the events in the reading you are preparing.)

Consider the Reading in the Context of the Liturgical Year

As previously discussed, each season has its own sense and flow that is evident in the readings. Reflect on where your reading occurs in relation to the weeks that have come before and will come after. What might be significant about when this reading falls in the season? How does that affect its message?

Praying with the Scripture

One of the best ways to prepare your reading is by praying through it and reflecting on it. This may seem obvious, but it can sometimes be easy to over-look the importance of praying with the Scriptures when you are worried about the mechanics of reading. Pope John Paul II reminded us of this in *Dies Domini*: "If Christian individuals and families are not regularly drawing new life from the reading of the sacred text in a spirit of prayer and docility to the church's interpretation, then it is difficult for the liturgical proclamation of the word of God alone to produce the fruit we might expect."[9]

Prayerful preparation also helps us to keep in mind that our Sunday gathering and our ministry within that sacred space is not about us or even about our community. Our prayer at the Sunday Eucharist is about what God did for us and continues to do for us through Jesus Christ. A prayerful, Christ-centered approach to Scripture will come across in your proclamation and will be a great service to the assembly.

Discern the Teaching in the Reading

Although this step in the preparation is similar to identifying the theme, point, or message of the passage, it is a bit more theologically specific. Does this text help us answer any of these questions?

- Who is God? Christ? the Holy Spirit?
- What is the nature of the Church? Sacraments? Salvation?
- How are disciples to act? How are we to make decisions ethically? How are we to serve and work?
- How are we to find hope? How are we to pray? How are we to be grateful and savor God's splendor?

Look up the Pronunciation of Words

Before you get much further in your preparation, it is important to identify what words are unfamiliar to you. Some of the names of people and places can be particularly difficult to pronounce, and yet their correct pronunciation is critical for the assembly to understand the reading. In that regard, there are several good pronunciation guides published in the United States; it is usually helpful to have one copy at home for practice, so that you aren't trying to learn the pronunciation a few minutes before Mass begins.

Incorrect pronunciations can undermine an otherwise fine proclamation. No matter how much authority you give to it with your voice, the line is not "A reading from the letter of Saint Paul to the *Philippines*," but rather "A reading from the letter of Saint Paul to the *Philippians*."

Pay particular attention to English words that are easily misread or mispronounced so that their meaning is not distorted for the assembly. For example, on the Third Sunday of Advent in year A, we should not hear from Isaiah: "Here is your God, he comes with *vindiction*"; rather, we should hear "Here is your God, he comes with *vindication*." By mispronouncing *vindication,* the assembly is left wondering what that word was and what it means, and they have missed the next sentences about God coming to save us and opening the eyes of the blind. Once you begin the proclamation during Mass, however, read

---

9. *Dies Domini,* 40.

everything with confidence and pronounce words that appear more than once in the text consistently so the assembly can follow you.

Use Public Speaking Techniques and Skills as You Practice

Once you have identified the genre, theme, and voice, looked at the background and context, discerned the teaching, prayed with the Scripture, and determined how to pronounce all the words, you need to continue practicing the reading aloud. Although your mind now understands the content, your mouth and tongue and voice have not yet become intimate with the text. Reading the words over and over will help them feel natural and familiar.

But first, be sure to "warm up." Just as singers would not open their mouths to sing publicly without first warming up their vocal chords, you should ensure that your voice is warmed up and your throat clear before you approach the ambo. First, take a few moments to open wide and close your mouth several times and move your jaw around. Be sure that you have taken some deep breaths to bring air into your lungs and have practiced controlled exhaling of those breaths with simple vowel sounds. Finally, it is often helpful to drink some water to ensure that there is no phlegm in your throat. These are the tried and true vocal warm-ups of international speaking organizations such as Toastmasters International, and they will serve you well to ensure that you do not need to begin by stepping up to the microphone and clearing your throat.[10]

Much practice helps you get inside your reading, and it can be helpful to practice in church at the ambo.

It can be helpful to record yourself reading and to read in front of a mirror. These methods will help you determine whether your voice is portraying the reading well and whether your facial expressions match your words.

Practice making your volume, pacing, emphasis, and voice quality appropriate for the Scripture. The work you have done to thoroughly know and understand this reading should be evident in your voice and face.

It is also helpful to ask someone to listen to you proclaim the reading and then reflect back to you what they heard in the proclamation. Do they hear what you are trying to convey? Thirty seconds after you have finished, can they tell you what the reading was about? If so, it is likely that your assembly will also hear what you are conveying. If not, try again.

---

10. These vocal techniques were adapted from Toastmasters International. Please refer to their website for additional information: www.toastmasters.org.

Over time, practicing again and again will help you to feel more comfortable with each reading and with your role as a reader. It will help you to be less self-conscious. If you struggle with "stage fright," practicing regularly will be a great help to you.

The skills that serve public speakers well are the same skills that serve readers well. These are not easy to master, and indeed people's expectations continue to grow as the many forms of popular media show us so many highly polished presenters.

As readers, we are not expected to be professional actors, but we are expected to take the role seriously and strive to always improve our presentation skills. In this way also we learn to become more transparent and allow God to be visible in the Word. If we mumble or speed through the reading, people will be distracted by us and miss how God is speaking to them. There are five areas in particular to which we should pay close attention in our presentation style.

CONTROL OF BREATH AND VOLUME

The way we breathe will control the phrasing of the reading and the volume at which it is proclaimed. Keeping our breathing deep and steady will also ensure that we stay calmer and more relaxed while we are reading. If you find yourself getting very nervous as you approach the ambo (or as you think about approaching the ambo), then take a few slow, deep breaths.

Remember that breathing should be done in the lungs and not in the head. This may sound silly, but when you are breathing fast and don't have enough breath to get through a full phrase, you are most likely taking shallow, short breaths. Even while reading, your breaths should fill your lungs so that you have enough air to make it through the phrases of the reading. Breathing at an inopportune time because you are out of air can change the meaning of a phrase. For example, if you are proclaiming the "Song of the Sea" from Exodus 15 during the Easter Vigil, there is a difference in meaning between these two phrasings:

> The flood waters covered them, / they sank into the depths [breath]
> like a stone. / Your right hand, O LORD, [breath]
> magnificent in power, / your right hand [breath]
> O Lord, has shattered the enemy.

versus

> The flood waters covered them, [breath]
>   they sank into the depths like a stone. [breath]
> Your right hand, O Lord, magnificent in power, [breath]
>   your right hand, O Lord, has shattered the enemy.

Exodus 15:5–6

The lectionary helps us with the phrasing of the readings by breaking them into "sense lines," lines that appear to be in a poetic format and show the reader how passages can be broken into phrases. Appropriate places for breath usually fall at the ends of some (but not all) sense lines. For this reason it's important to practice with a preparation aid that presents the reading as it looks in the lectionary—in sense lines.[11]

Your breathing will also control the volume of your proclamation. Controlling the volume is not just about using the microphone well or being loud, though both are important. It is also about making sure that you are speaking from the air in your chest rather than from the air in your nose. This feeling of speaking at a lower part of the body will help you keep the pitch in a lower and more authoritative part of your voice, and it will help you project your voice rather than just shout. Although shouting is rarely called for in Scripture proclamation, projecting your voice loudly is often appropriate, particularly when there is a great deal of ambient noise in the worship space. Breathing deeply and speaking from your filled lungs will give you the ability to increase the volume, project your voice, and have enough breath to get through full phrases in the reading.

CLEAR ARTICULATION AND PRONUNCIATION

Enunciating words clearly is extremely important for the reader. Make sure that all syllables are pronounced, that the endings of words are not dropped, and that multiple words are not strung together to form one unintelligible word.

This helps the assembly to hear and understand the Word of God. Particularly when so many of our communities have a variety of nationalities among both their reader and assembly members, it is critical for everyone's understanding that there be no mumbling or slurring of words.

We've already discussed the importance of pronouncing words properly. Correct pronunciation allows the assembly to follow the reading and not wonder what it is you really meant to say.

APPROPRIATE PACING OF THE READING

The first principle concerning the pacing of the reading is to slow down. It is rare that a new reader reads too slowly for people to understand the meaning of the text. Reading at a conversational pace is too fast.

While you may feel that you are reading painfully slow, this will most likely not be the case. Beyond slowing down, the pace of the reading depends on the text, the space, and the sound system.

In each reading there will be points where a pause is needed to emphasize what has just been said. Studying the reading will help you identify those

---

11. *Workbook for Lectors, Gospel Readers, and Proclaimers of the Word*® is a very helpful resource for this task. See page 63 of the resource section.

pause points. In other places, the sense of the text will be expressed better by a faster pace. The effect of repetitions may stand out better when spoken more quickly, but a slower pace helps people hear each phrase.

Besides pacing a reading to help enhance its meaning, you need to understand the space in which you are proclaiming the reading and the sound system that you are using. In a large church with tile floors, there will be a delay between the sound made by the reader and the sound heard by the people all the way in the back of the church. There may also be an echo. Most churches present some acoustical challenges for the reader. Practicing in the church with the reader trainer will help you determine how long your pauses need to be to allow the words you have spoken to reach everyone. The sound system will also affect this. Some very large churches have two speakers in the front of the church and none anywhere else. Other (mostly newer) churches have installed sound systems that provide almost instantaneous sound to everyone in the church at the same time. Either way, there will probably be an echo that you must let die between paragraphs or individual points in a reading. Again, your trainer will help you master the sound system and the challenges of the building.

Tone of voice and emphasis will help you express the meaning of the reading.

EFFECTIVE VOICE QUALITY AND EMPHASIS

Your preparation of the reading will help you understand the mood and tone of the reading and what needs to be emphasized. What you emphasize in a phrase can potentially change its meaning for people hearing it, so the decision should be made carefully. Once you are extremely familiar with the reading and have a good sense of what God is conveying in it, you will be much more comfortable deciding exactly what tone to use and where to place emphasis.

As you consider your voice quality, be careful to keep your voice coming from your lungs and chest, and at a lower, more authoritative tone. Even in readings of great gladness and rejoicing, allowing the pitch of your voice to be high will make it harder for people to hear and understand what you are saying. You can speak in the lower part of your voice with a smile on your face, and the joy will come out in the quality of your vocal expression.

Vocal expression is essential for conveying meaning in the reading. Although expression can cross the line into the overly dramatic, distracting from the message of the reading, most readers use too little rather than too much expression. The challenge is to make your proclamation expressive so that it draws the assembly into the reading and conveys its meaning effectively.

Practice at Church

A great deal of the preparation we have discussed can be done anywhere. However, it is extremely important, especially as a new reader, that you practice your proclamation in the church. This includes practicing everything you will do as a reader from the opening procession through the closing procession.

As with the pacing of the reading, the sound system will make a difference in how the reading comes across. Each sound system is different, and your trainer will need to explain the particulars of your parish system to you. The microphone will be either *omnidirectional* and pick up sound from all sides (in which case it does not need to be moved up or down to accommodate your height), or *unidirectional* and only pick up what is spoken directly into it (in which case you will need to move it directly in front of your mouth). Some microphones are hypersensitive, causing a popping sound when the letters *p* or *b* are voiced or hissing with the letter *s*. In that case you will need to learn to adjust to it. Sound systems are designed to increase volume, but you must learn to project your voice well so that you can truly control the expression of the reading and not simply make it louder or softer.

You will also need to be comfortable with the physical setting of the church. You need to know where exactly to sign in when you arrive, where to wait for the opening procession, what path the opening procession will take, where readers are to sit, and how you are to move to and from the ambo. Practicing the movements around the space—all the movements in the reader's routine—will make you much less self-conscious or nervous or both.

Most parishes will rehearse all of this with you at least once or twice before you are assigned to be the lector at a Mass. However, if you find that you are not comfortable after those practices, do not be afraid to ask to come back and practice again. In some churches, you might be allowed to come in when the church is not in use and it is convenient for you, walk through all the motions in the space, and practice the reading from the ambo. It's definitely worth asking what you can arrange. Over time, you will begin to feel comfortable with the space, and will be able to focus your energies not on where to go or what to do next, but on proclaiming the scriptures as well as you can.

Pay Attention to Nonverbal Communication

While we have discussed most extensively the verbal aspects of proclaiming Scripture at Mass, your nonverbal communication is also extremely important.

First, it is important to have good posture, whether you are processing or standing at the ambo. Slouching will detract from your reading, as will leaning back and putting your hands in your pockets. Hold your shoulders back, place your legs directly beneath your shoulders (don't lock your knees!), and keep your back straight. This alert, dignified posture will convey the significance of the proclamation. However, take care not to throw your shoulders too far back and your chest too far out so that you project an air of arrogance instead of humility and dignity. Practicing in front of a mirror will help you find the posture that looks and feels appropriate.

While reading from the ambo, it is important to make eye contact with the assembly. The opening line and closing dialogue of the reading can easily be done while looking at the people. It is also important to look at people during the reading. This really does help to keep people engaged and help to convey meaning. You may feel most comfortable making eye contact with the assembly members throughout the reading, as long as you are familiar enough with it to be able to look up at the people and back down at the lectionary without losing your place.

All postures and gestures should be done with care and deliberation. The gesture you are most likely to make is a profound bow from the waist if you pass in front of the altar on your way to or from the ambo. (There is no reason to bow if you do not pass in front of the altar). Good liturgical gesture is done with grace and meaning. In general, hand gestures are not appropriate when reading; they are too distracting. So that your hands have a natural place to be, let them rest on the ambo, holding the lectionary, or subtly marking your place with a finger.

All of your movements should be done with purpose and reverence, whether walking to or from the ambo, or bowing before the altar. Movements should be neither too fast nor too slow. When standing at the ambo, be still and avoid fidgeting. Shifting your weight back and forth from one foot to the other, or slightly bouncing up and down, will distract greatly from your reading. Often these are nervous gestures we are not aware of, so feedback from others is particularly helpful in determining if we have a problem that needs correction.

If you are carrying the *Book of the Gospels* in the opening procession, or removing the lectionary after the second reading, it is important that you handle these books reverently. Apart from the readings within them, the books themselves, especially the *Book of the Gospels*, are symbols of our faith and of the salvation of Christ throughout the history of God's people. They should be carried with two hands and picked up and put down carefully.

Finally, your choice of attire also says something about your ministry and the importance of us gathering in praise and worship of our Lord. Some churches have dress codes for readers and some do not. If your parish does have a dress code, be sure that you follow it. If not, there are some basic principles that should guide your clothing selections. First, most likely you will be notified in advance when you will be serving as a reader, a leader within the community. Therefore, you should be dressed so as to convey the message that you knew you were coming to serve and cared about that service to the people and to God. In this case, blue jeans, shorts, or T-shirts are inappropriate attire. Second, your clothing should never distract from your ministry. If you have bare shoulders, a bare midriff, an excessively low neckline, tight clothing, or colors far brighter than is customary for your community, most people in the assembly will spend more energy looking at you than listening to the reading. This takes away from all the preparation you have put into your ministry and makes it difficult for people to hear the Word of God from you. Avoid this kind of distraction by giving some thought to what clothes in your wardrobe would be most appropriate, keeping in mind that simplicity, modesty, and dignity are your goals.

The Reader's Role during Mass

The reader's tasks may vary from parish to parish. They depend on whether there is a deacon, how many readers are assigned to a Mass, and so forth. What follows is a general overview. It is important that you know about any variations at your parish before you begin your ministry.

Our first responsibility as a reader is to arrive early (fifteen to twenty minutes before the start of Mass, or at whatever time your parish directs) and to sign in. This is important because it ensures that people are in place ahead of time and there is no last-minute wondering *whether* you are going to arrive. This also allows you to check in, greet the other ministers, go to the ambo and ensure that you know exactly where in the lectionary your reading is, adjust the microphone, pray silently before Mass, and prepare yourself mentally to serve the community well. Depending on your personal temperament, you may need even more time to prepare yourself than your church requires. Feel free to come as early as is helpful. Coming later than asked, however, makes both you and the other ministers rushed, anxious, and unfocused for the liturgy. Do your utmost to avoid this.

At many parishes, readers will be a part of the opening procession. If this is not the case in your parish, you should be in your seat five minutes before Mass so that you are ready to go. If you will be a part of the opening procession, however, you should gather with the other ministers and be ready for that role whenever you are asked to be there, or at least five minutes before Mass begins.

The opening procession will be led by the altar server with the incense if it is used, next the cross bearer and candle bearers, and then the readers. If there is no deacon and your parish has a *Book of the Gospels*, then you may be asked to carry it in procession. If so, you will follow the other reader and hold the book slightly elevated (not with arms straight above your head, but in front

If a deacon is not present, a lay reader carries the Book of the Gospels.

of you and slightly higher than your face; see the photo on page 40). When the procession reaches the sanctuary, you and the other ministers will make a profound bow to the altar and proceed to your place. If you are carrying the *Book of the Gospels*, however, omit the bow, walk behind the altar, facing toward the assembly, place the *Book of the Gospels* there reverently, and proceed to your seat.[12]

After the collect (opening prayer) is concluded, the assembly will sit down. At this point, the priest celebrant may offer a few words of introduction to the readings. If there is a children's Liturgy of the Word, the children will be dismissed at this point. It is important to know if there will be something happening after the opening prayer and before the first reading. Once the assembly is seated and settled, the first reader proceeds to the ambo. The lectionary has already been placed there, open to the first reading. Take a moment before beginning to ensure that people are ready to listen.

The ritual language that begins the reading is very important: "A reading from the . . . " It is not appropriate to begin in any other way or with any other words. The lectionary will have the introductory words at the top of the reading. In a clear and firm voice, proclaim exactly what the lectionary specifies. Then pause for a moment. If at all possible, this should be done while looking

---

12. In some areas, the reader may be seated in the sanctuary. It is best to consult your pastoral leadership staff or office for divine worship to determine local practice. If the readers are seated in the sanctuary, then they will join in the closing procession. If the readers return to their pew, they will not join in the closing procession.

at the people, and not at the lectionary. Because of your preparation before the Mass, you will know exactly what book the reading is from.

At the end of the reading it is appropriate to pause for a moment, look up, and address the assembly with these words: "The word of the Lord." Wait for the assembly's response. It is customary in many places to pause for a few moments of silence and proceed back to your seat, but follow your parish's guidelines.

The psalmist should allow a bit of silence after the reader sits down, so that people can remember and reflect on the word they have just heard. The length of that silence will depend on the parish, although a good rule of thumb is to wait at least the length of a mentally recited Hail Mary. This recitation should be prayerful and meditative—not rushed. An exact length is not specified, but it is important for all ministers to be comfortable with silence. The more we readers are comfortable with silence, the more the assembly will also be comfortable with silence.

> The Liturgy of the Word is to be celebrated in such a way as to favor meditation, and so any kind of haste such as hinders recollection is clearly to be avoided. In the course of it, brief periods of silence are also appropriate, accommodated to the assembled congregation; by means of these, under the action of the Holy Spirit, the Word of God may be grasped by the heart and a response through prayer may be prepared. It may be appropriate to observe such periods of silence, for example, before the Liturgy of the Word itself begins, after the First and Second Reading, and lastly at the conclusion of the Homily.[13]

The psalmist will proceed to the ambo for the proclamation of the psalm. While this is a Scripture reading, ritual language (such as "A reading from Psalm . . .") does not precede it. Instead, the psalmist begins with the response and then, with a gesture, invites the assembly to repeat the response. At the end of the psalm, the psalmist returns to his or her place. Please note that "it is preferable for the Responsorial Psalm to be sung."[14] "The Christian faithful who come together as one in expectation of the Lord's coming are instructed by the Apostle Paul to sing together Psalms, hymns, and spiritual canticles (cf. Col. 3:16)."[15] If a cantor is not available, however, then a reader may recite the psalm.

When the psalmist has returned to his or her place, the reader proclaiming the second reading will again allow a short pause, rise, and go to the ambo. The same instructions apply for the second reading as for the first. After the assembly has responded to that reading with "Thanks be to God," pause for a few moments before being seated. If the community has a *Book of the Gospels*,

---

13. GIRM, 56.
14. GIRM, 61.
15. GIRM, 39.

the reader may need to move the lectionary to a lower shelf of the ambo or to a nearby table or seat, depending on the arrangements of the parish.

Again, it is appropriate to observe a few moments of silence following the second reading. As the Gospel acclamation begins, the assembly stands. If there is a Gospel procession, it may include incense, candles, and the *Book of the Gospels*. Once at the ambo, the Gospel reader (the deacon or, if no deacon is present, a priest) enacts a ritual dialogue with the assembly:

> *Deacon/Priest: The Lord be with you.*
> **People: And with your spirit.**

> *Deacon/Priest: A reading from the holy Gospel according to N.*
> **People: Glory to you, O Lord.**

On a very solemn occasion, the deacon or priest may then incense the *Book of the Gospels* before proceeding with the reading. At the conclusion of the Gospel, the assembly is seated, the *Book of the Gospels* is left on the ambo, and the homily follows.

After the homily there is a third period of silence so that the people have a chance to reflect prayerfully on what they have heard. Then the assembly stands for the profession of faith. As this ends, the universal prayer (or prayer of the faithful) begins. If there is a deacon at the Mass, he should read the prayers from the ambo or "another suitable place."[16] If not, and this role falls to you, move to the ambo or "another suitable place"[17] for the proclamation of the prayers. They are read clearly, and everyone responds with the spoken or sung response.

Before proclaiming the Gospel, the deacon or priest engages the people in a ritual dialogue.

Only after the priest celebrant has read the concluding prayer for the universal prayer do you leave the ambo and return to your seat.

Reading the universal prayer is also a significant part of your ministry. "In the Universal Prayer or Prayer of the Faithful, the people respond in some sense to the Word of God which they have received in faith and, exercising the office of their baptismal Priesthood, offer prayers to God for the salvation of all."[18] Practice these prayers in advance so that they do not sound like announcements, but the true expression of the people's petitions. There is often a petition for those who are sick or those who have died that will include one or more

---

16. GIRM, 71.
17. GIRM, 71.
18. GIRM, 69.

names. The community prays for these people because they are a part of the Body of Christ and their presence or absence affects us all. It is important that their names are pronounced correctly and are recognizable to the assembly, so be sure to ask someone in authority if you are unsure how to pronounce a name. It is a great privilege to proclaim the prayer of the entire community, and your preparation should reflect this.

As the Liturgy of the Eucharist begins, the role of the reader is finished in most parishes. The *Book of the Gospels* is not processed out of the church at the end of Mass.

Responding to Difficult or Unusual Situations

No matter how well prepared you are for your ministry, every now and then something out of the ordinary will happen. The first principle for all ministers is to stay calm. The most outrageous situations are easier for the entire assembly to deal with if those they perceive as leaders (including you as a reader) remain calm, composed, and keep a sense of reverence about what they are doing. It is also especially important that we always exhibit a sense of hospitality and charity. This is sometimes easier said than done, but it is important to keep in mind.

Listed below are some of the more likely difficult or unusual situations to come up. It is by no means an exhaustive list, because if we knew everything that was going to happen, we wouldn't be surprised by it. These examples will give you a few principles for making wise decisions on how to deal with events in the immediacy of the moment. We always pray that the Spirit will be with us in such moments, leading us to respond in the most loving and helpful ways.

Restless Children

Children and noise are, thankfully, a part of most of our assemblies. They remind us of young life and hope that is constantly growing in our communities. When you are trying to proclaim Scripture, however, they can sometimes be distracting for both you and the assembly. It is occasionally helpful to pause for a moment and allow excess noise to die down, particularly before you begin a reading. When this does not work, it may become necessary to project your voice slightly more forcefully into the microphone. If this is not enough, then you must simply go on as best you can.

There are a few times a year when we know in advance that the church is going to be especially loud: Christmas Time and Easter Time. On these occasions when there are many visitors and a larger than usual assembly, it is a good idea to have a special rehearsal to prepare readers for the higher noise level. At that time, the readers are to gather and practice their readings from the ambo, with the sound system on, while the other readers try to approximate the sort of noise level that might be expected in the church. This will allow the liturgy coordinator to set the microphone levels at a slightly higher than normal volume if possible, and will allow you to be prepared to proclaim the Scripture well, without being distracted by the extra noise around you.

Distracting or Alarming Interruptions

If you are in the middle of a reading and there is a sudden loud noise from outside the building (such as sirens passing by), it is generally helpful to pause for a few seconds and then resume where you stopped, as long as this will not interrupt a sentence or phrase. If the pause would be awkward, then the best course of action would be to get louder for a few moments during the distraction and lower your voice again once it passes.

Every now and then there will be a sudden commotion in the church. Standing at the ambo, you may notice it, even though the majority of the assembly does not. If it is a small commotion in one area, then it is best to simply continue with the reading. If, however, someone yells for help and everyone turns to see what is going on, the priest celebrant should attend to what is happening, and you should wait for him to tell you that it is time to continue. At that point it is usually best to begin the reading from the beginning.

Other Responsibilities of a Reader

The priest, liturgical ministers, and indeed the entire assembly depend on you to be present for your ministry. Readers are generally scheduled in advance for specific readings at specific Masses on specific days. You are responsible for ensuring that you know when you are scheduled, and that you are prepared for and present for those Masses. If you cannot participate in a particular Mass for which you are scheduled, it is your responsibility to find a substitute from among the other readers at your parish. If this is not possible, inform the coordinator of readers as soon as possible so that other arrangements can be made.

At particular Masses and at all times, you exercise your ministry as a responsible, collaborative, and encouraging team member. You try to be a good communicator, to be helpful to other readers and to other liturgical ministers. You also model active participation for the assembly.

Finally, regardless of how long you have been a reader or how confident you feel about your skills at the ministry, you are responsible for ensuring that you receive ongoing formation. This can take many forms, including advanced public speaking courses and additional Scripture studies. However you choose to continue to grow in this ministry, it is important to remember that the assembly is always counting on you to continue to bring life and meaning to the text you are proclaiming.

Overall, it is a very straightforward ministry, and the better you are prepared for it, the simpler and more transparent it will appear to those gathered in worship. But there is real work that needs to go into making the practiced and carefully considered delivery appear simple and truly transparent. As St. Benedict wrote in his Rule, "The reader should not be the one who just happens to pick up the book, but someone who will read for a whole week, beginning on Sunday. . . . Brothers will read and sing, not according to rank, but according to their ability to benefit their hearers."[19]

A day of reflection on the Word could provide readers with time for self assessment.

Reflection and Self-Assessment

As important as it is to prepare well for proclaiming the Sacred Scripture, it is equally important to reflect on your proclamation immediately afterward to assess the effect of your proclamation. Neither preparation nor reflection is effective without the other. During your service as a reader over the coming years, you will find that if you are to serve the assembly well and continue to grow in your ministry, neither can be eliminated—even if you are tempted to think you know what you're doing and have done it all before. Use these questions for self-asessment to guide you in this process.

Questions for Self-Assessment

1. Did I feel prepared and ready to serve the community?

2. Did I understand my reading and have a sense of the message or teaching I was conveying to the assembly?

3. Did the quality of my voice, expression, pacing, and emphasis feel right? Were there things I would do differently now?

4. Did the amount and timing of eye contact feel appropriate?

5. Were there areas of the reading where I stumbled? If so, do I know why?

6. What did I feel good about that I would like to be sure to remember in the future?

7. Do I have a sense that I ministered to the community well and that I can do so again in the future?

---

19. *Rule of Saint Benedict*, 38.

Even more helpful is the practice of group feedback with other readers that should be a part of all of our ministries. These sessions should occur regularly, perhaps monthly or bimonthly, so that the work of the reader and the appropriate feedback are not forgotten over a span of several months.

It can seem quite daunting to present yourself to a group for their reactions to work you care about. But honest feedback is one of the best means we have of learning and growing in our ministry. Group feedback sessions with other readers allow people to say to one another, "This is how you helped me to understand what you were proclaiming, and this is what got in the way." The members of the group should always speak with respect and with the intent of giving useful information as a way of encouraging each other. Group feedback also helps us gauge the effectiveness of our proclamation. Without input from others, it is hard to know how well God's Word is truly being received by the assembly. And when we take the time to critically listen to others and participate in their reflection processes, we can pick up on the good characteristics of their proclamation styles and learn from their mistakes as well as our own.

When engaging in a group feedback process, it is most helpful for participants to speak as members of the assembly about what helped or hindered their experience of the reading, rather than try to take the role of a teacher or judge. For example, giving a fellow reader feedback about how his pacing led you to interpret the meaning of the passage (which might or might not have been the meaning the reader intended to convey) would be helpful. Telling a reader that you weren't able to hear the last words of several of the lines because her voice trailed off would be helpful. Telling a fellow reader that his or her attire or posture distracted you from hearing the Scripture could also be helpful. Using evaluative terms such as *good*, *weak*, or *ok* simply isn't that helpful, because those words are vague and don't describe the effect that a particular element in the proclamation had on the listener. Questions for the group feedback session will help focus the exercise.

Questions for a Group Feedback Session

1. Were you able to hear and make sense of the reading? Was the volume of the reader's voice strong enough?

2. Could you recognize all the words from the reader's articulation? Were any of the pronunciations of the words unfamiliar?

3. How did the pace allow you to listen and follow?

4. How did the quality of the voice express the mood of the reading? What tone or meaning did it convey to you?

5. Was the nonverbal communication (posture, eye contact, movements, attire) helpful or distracting?

Overall, if readers gather together and are open to the process of feedback, it will help all of them grow in their ministry and in their understanding of the effect of their ministry on others. This is a tremendous gift!

Questions for Reflection and Discussion

1. What has drawn you to serve as reader in the liturgy? Did you find a particular love for the Scriptures over time or recently? How do you hope to share that love for the Scriptures with others through your ministry? What aspects of the liturgy have called you into liturgical ministry?

2. How do you hope to personally grow and develop in your faith through this ministry?

3. Think of readers whom you find particularly effective in their proclamation. What is it about their ministry that touches you? What skills of theirs do you wish to emulate in your own ministry?

4. As you begin your ministry, what study and preparation can you commit yourself to on a regular basis?

Chapter Four

Spirituality and Discipleship

The Spirit of the Lord is upon me.

—*Luke 4:18*

The reader is the mouthpiece through which God speaks to the Church. Readers are effective when they open their ears to hear God's Word and open their hearts to love God's people.

Readers take care of their spirit. Just as athletes care for their bodies, teachers train their minds, musicians practice to refine their art, and firefighters rehearse procedures for safety, so readers spend time with the Spirit. Being a reader is not just having a ministry—it is being a certain kind of person.

Nurturing your spirit gives God more ways to use you. You will be God's servant in ways beyond imagining.

The Spirituality of Sunday Mass

The most important activity of your life is your regular participation at Sunday Mass. You do not have to be a reader to know this is true.

Sunday is the Lord's Day, the day when we commemorate the rising of Christ from the dead. Our celebration of the Eucharist expresses our belief in the resurrection of Christ, and our hope that one day we shall share glory with him in the Father. To participate in Mass is to take a stand for our belief in God, who created our life, who sent Jesus into the world, and who promised the Holy Spirit, the giver of charity. Sunday belongs to the Lord; we devote our time to God.

Sunday is also a day of leisure. It should feel different from other days. People often say it should not be hard to set aside one hour a week for God. That is true, but a fruitful celebration of Mass will require more time. It will take time for leisure, especially before Mass. It will be hard to participate if we are busy up to the time we leave home to go to church. Our minds and bodies need time to prepare. You don't exercise without first stretching. You don't have heat in the car until it warms up. The time before Mass is spent preparing our minds and hearts for what we soon will do. We will place ourselves in God's presence, concentrate on the words and gestures of the service, and form a community of believers.

While you are at church, even if you are not serving as reader that day, put your heart, will, mind, and strength into the Eucharist. As a member of the assembly, you will be called upon to sing songs, make responses, assume postures, make gestures, and observe silences. As a reader, you are a leader,

As a reader, you help to form the community at Sunday Mass.

a model for the behavior of others. People will do what you do. If you model participation and prayer for them even when you are not in the ambo, they will more gratefully follow your words when you are.

You are responsible for helping to form the community at Sunday Mass. While you speak, all will listen as one body. You can also help to form this community by getting to know the other people at church. Spend some time before and after Mass visiting with people and getting to know how they are. If you are not good at names, practice them. Obtain a parish directory. After Mass, make a note about the people you met today, so you can seek them out the next time.

It takes time to learn the names of people in a parish, but it is worth the effort. You will feel more and more at home at church, and people will feel more and more at home with you as their reader. Especially if part of your ministry is to lead the petitions for the universal prayer, you will want to know how to pray for the people you lead. You will come to learn their joys and sorrows. You bring all these with you into the ambo. There, as you read, you proclaim a word that challenges and comforts, that makes people question and offers them hope. There, as you pray, you sense more urgently the concerns the community needs to lift to God.

Sunday Mass is the most important activity of your week. There you give your heart to God and lend an ear to your neighbor. There you praise God for the gift of life and resurrection, and you work at forming the community of believers who put their trust in God.

Cultivating Spirituality through the Lectionary

The Bible makes a good companion for every Christian's prayer. The lectionary can be an especially good prayer resource for the reader.

Years ago, Catholics were actually discouraged from reading the Bible. Authorities were afraid that people would misinterpret what it says. Catholics used their Bibles as record books in which the names of children, the choice of spouses, and the dates of death were entered. They rested on coffee tables or nearby shelves. But rarely did Catholics use Bibles for prayer.

It is fitting to commend the names of the family to pages of the Bible. But it is more fitting to read the Word of God.

Today, the Catholic Church includes a wider variety of Scripture readings in a typical Sunday Mass than in the past. Readings from Scripture form an integral part of our worship outside of Mass as well. As a Church we have recommitted ourselves to the Word of God, and many individuals have discovered its beauty as well—in the Liturgy of the Hours, for example, and in liturgies of the Word.

For readers, a lectionary offers an ideal way to use the Bible for prayer and study. (Paperback study editions can be purchased; see page 63 in the resource section.) The lectionary is the collection of readings used for Mass and other principal celebrations of the Church. It does not include every line of the Bible. It does include those parts of the Bible deemed most useful for Christians to know, arranged in a helpful way. It doesn't look like an abridged Bible, but in a way, it is.

Although readers can find out which readings are appointed for any given Sunday by consulting any number of different tools, it would be good for readers to learn how the lectionary is organized.

If you do not own your own, take a look at the one in church sometime. The lectionary requires four volumes. The first is the one you use the most. It contains the readings for Sunday. The second and third volumes are used for weekdays, and the fourth has collected the readings for other special occasions.

Sundays

The first volume, though, is the one you should know the best. Notice that the book is arranged by seasons: Advent, Christmas Time, Lent, Easter Time, and Ordinary Time. There is a section for solemnities of the Lord during Ordinary Time, where you find the readings for days like the Most Holy Trinity and the Most Holy Body and Blood of Christ. Many readers find these readings difficult to locate.

Each Sunday offers readings for years A, B, and C. If the number of the calendar year is divisible exactly by three, then we are in year C. You can figure out year A and B from there. Many ritual editions of the lectionary place all the

Sunday readings for each year in separate volumes—A, B, and C. The liturgical year begins, of course, with the Advent that precedes the new calendar year.

Weekdays

On weekdays during Ordinary Time, the first reading is on a two-year cycle, but the Gospel remains the same each year. At the beginning of Ordinary Time, the lectionary presents a semi-continuous reading of Mark, considered to be the oldest of the four Gospels. It then moves to Matthew and concludes with Luke. During the liturgical seasons of the year (Advent, Christmas Time, Lent, and Easter Time), we hear the same first reading each year and the same Gospel reading. Excerpts from the Gospel according to John are proclaimed during these seasons, especially during the second half of Lent and throughout Easter Time. To simplify things for the reader, the readings of each year are kept in separate ritual books. We use year I readings in odd-numbered years and year II readings in even-numbered years. Years I and II begin with the Advent that precedes the odd- and even-numbered calendar years, respectively.

Special Occasions

The fourth volume contains the readings for special occasions: marriages, funerals, baptisms, and a host of other events. If you are ever looking for a particular passage from the Bible to fit a certain circumstance, it is worth looking at this volume. You may not find the exact theme you need, but once you become familiar with the contents of the book, it will be easier to locate useful passages.

Navigating through the Lectionary

In the front of the lectionary you will find several tables.[1] One of them shows you which lectionary cycle falls during which year. It also gives the date for some moveable feasts such as Ash Wednesday, Easter, and Pentecost. It will tell you how many weeks of Ordinary Time will fall between the Christmas season and Lent. It will also say which week of Ordinary Time will resume on what day when the Easter season is over.

Another table gives the order of the second readings in Ordinary Time. If you're interested, you can see at a glance which books of the Bible you will be reading during Ordinary Time this year.

In the second appendix of the lectionary is a complete chart of readings found in the lectionary. It is arranged according to the books of the Bible, starting with Genesis and ending with Revelation. If you know a citation and you wonder where to find it in the four-volume lectionary, you can look it up in the second appendix.

One of the more important skills a reader can develop is how to figure out why a particular reading is chosen for any given day. You can find some help for

---

1. These tables appear in the *front* of the ritual edition of the lectionary, but at the *back* of the study edition.

It can be helpful to talk with other readers about the meaning of the texts you will proclaim on a particular Sunday.

this in the lectionary, but you often have to use your imagination. You will find a most helpful introduction to the lectionary in the front of the first volume. Chapter 4 is called "The General Arrangement of Readings for Mass," and chapter 5 is the "Description of the Order of Readings." Paragraphs 64 through 68 explain the principles behind the choice of texts for Sundays. Paragraphs 92 through 110 explain the rationale behind the choice of readings season by season.

Readers familiar with these principles will understand another layer beneath the Scripture they read. They certainly want to come to know the meaning of the passage as it appears in the Bible—what book it is from, what part of the narrative it tells, what problems it is answering, or what part of an extended argument it makes. But they will also want to know the meaning of this passage as it appears in the lectionary. Why was it chosen for this particular day? Does it have a theme that relates to the Gospel? Is there a word or phrase that sounds the theme of the season of the year we are in? Is it simply a continuation of a passage we heard last Sunday? Answers to these questions are critical if the reader is to nuance the reading in a way that lends coherence to the entire Liturgy of the Word.

For this reason, it will help you to have some familiarity with all the scriptures of any given Sunday, even those you do not proclaim, including the psalm. The psalm is often chosen as a direct response to the first reading. If you will be reading the first reading, consider why the psalm for that day fits. What will the Gospel be, and how does it fulfill the ideas germinating in your text? If you see how all the readings of a given day interrelate, you will read with greater understanding.

By spending time studying the lectionary, you are deepening your appreciation of the spiritual task you do. Your love for the Word of God will grow as you become more familiar with the way our Church proclaims it and hears it.

Prayer at Home

Everyone is encouraged to pray at home. The early Christians made it a habit twice a day—morning and evening. If it was getting light or getting dark, it was getting to be time to pray.

Do you set aside some time at home for prayer? What resources do you use? Do you incorporate passages from the Bible? Are the Sunday scriptures part of your weekly prayer?

Many readers like to make the lectionary part of their prayer at home. If you know the citations for the weekday readings, for example, you could read one or more of them as part of your meal prayer. Or, in anticipation of the weekend, you could read the coming Sunday scriptures throughout the week. You could read one a day, including the psalm. Or you could read more than one a day and repeat them at other meals. The more you hear the Word of God, the more it can penetrate your very being.

One method of praying the scriptures has traditionally been called *lectio divina.* It is a process of slow meditation on the Word of God. When you read the morning paper or an assignment for class or a light novel, you probably do it as quickly as you can. But *lectio divina* is a slow reading of the Word of God. Try the following. Calm yourself and prepare your heart to acquire an attitude of prayer. Read slowly the passage you are going to proclaim on Sunday. Did something in the text grab your attention? Reflect a while on that word or phrase. Memorize it. Pray about it: tell God what is on your mind about those words. Then rest in the presence of God, who comes to you in this word. Read the passage slowly again, and let it speak to you more deeply than it did the first time.

Take some time with these scriptures. Some people like to journal. Find a quiet place and time at home. Read over the scriptures for this coming week. Jot down a few thoughts about them. Return to the same readings later on. Write some more. How is God speaking to you personally through these readings? Before you present these readings to the entire community, have you wrestled with them yourself? Before you shoulder the job of saying God's Word to others, have you asked yourself, What is God saying to me?

Some people like a more structured prayer, such as the Liturgy of the Hours. Morning and Evening Prayer are especially beautiful. They give you a generous helping of psalms and canticles for your reflection, as well as a short Scripture passage during each prayer. But don't let the brevity of this passage mislead you. It contains only a few words, so that you can hear them, meditate on them, and act on them. There are many ways to pray with the Word of God.

Spiritual Reading about Scripture

Many people who have studied the Bible in depth have authored commentaries on the various books of Scripture. Such a book can help you understand more of the passages you read and feed you great insights. There are good overviews of the entire Bible, as well as journals dedicated to biblical studies. These are written on a variety of levels. Some require very little previous understanding of the Bible. Others are for more devoted scholars.

Treat yourself to a good book about the Bible or a commentary on a part of the Bible that appeals to you. Read it in small doses and let it nourish your appreciation of God's Word.

Retreat Days

Look for opportunities to learn more about the Bible. There may be a retreat center near where you live. Take advantage of the days they offer for prayer and meditation. Attend a retreat of several days once a year if you are able. Take a spiritual book or a biblical commentary with you to a special place where you can spend some time reading slowly with understanding.

Pay attention to how other people use Scripture. How did the homilist preach about the readings this week? Did the message surprise you? If you heard a spiritual talk this week, how did the speaker quote Scripture? Which passages were used? Why? Which words of the Bible are quoted in articles you read or songs you sing?

Spiritual Conversation

When you have spiritual conversation with others, rely on the scriptures for help. When someone shares his or her joys or sorrows with you, think for a few moments about the Bible. Is there something in the life of Jesus that reminds you of what this person is going through? Is there some story from the Old Testament or a passage from the epistles that sheds light on this situation? Is there a psalm that captures the spirit of what this person is going through?

Challenge yourself to name a passage from the Bible that applies to different situations in life. It will increase your familiarity with the Bible and your ability to relate it to the various emotional phases we undergo.

Prayers

Prayers you may find helpful are offered here and at the beginning and end of the book.

If a priest is to read the Gospel at Mass, he says this before he begins: "Almighty God, cleanse my heart and my lips that I may worthily proclaim your Gospel."

After the reading, the deacon or the priest says, "May the words of the Gospel wipe away our sins."

Several of the psalms sing praise to God's Word. Psalm 19 is one that may be sung at the Easter Vigil. The refrain for this particular responsory comes from a story in the Gospel according to John. Some disciples were turning away from Jesus because they could not accept his teaching on the Eucharist. Jesus was afraid even the Twelve would go. But Peter spoke on behalf of the others: "Lord, you have the words of everlasting life."[2]

This lovely sentiment is paired with a psalm honoring the law of God, the sacred Torah, the holy word in which we find all wisdom. The psalm is filled with synonyms for God's word: law, decree, precepts, command, and ordinances. They are sweeter than honey.

Responsorial Psalm   *Psalm 19:8, 9, 10, 11*

R: Lord, you have the words of everlasting life.

> The law of the LORD is perfect,
>   refreshing the soul;
> the decree of the Lord is trustworthy,
>   giving wisdom to the simple.

R: Lord, you have the words of everlasting life.

> The precepts of the Lord are right,
>   rejoicing the heart;
> the command of the Lord is clear,
>   enlightening the eye.

R: Lord, you have the words of everlasting life.

> The fear of the Lord is pure,
>   enduring forever;
> the ordinances of the Lord are true,
>   all of them just.

R: Lord, you have the words of everlasting life.

> They are more precious than gold,
>   than a heap of purest gold;
> sweeter also than syrup
>   or honey from the comb.

R: Lord, you have the words of everlasting life.

---

2. See John 6:68c. See also Psalm 19 from the Easter Vigil (*Lectionary for Mass*, #41ABC).

Cultivating Spirituality through Service

Every Christian is called to serve others, and the reader should be especially prepared to do so. Your service at the ambo is not about you. It is about the Word of God. Throughout your life, you strive to decrease, so that Christ may increase in you. When people hear you read, they will hear God speak. And when people see you act, they should see Christ act.

You probably already offer service to others in a variety of ways—to your family, your neighbors, people at church, at work, and even to complete strangers. But you might give some thought to types of service that especially fit your ministry as a reader.

When do you read the Bible to others? Might you make yourself available to read at parish funerals when bereaved families do not have family members who wish to read— or at infant baptisms that take place outside of Mass? Would residents at a nursing home or hospital like you to read passages for them? Would the catechumens in your parish like to know how you prepare to read and what the Word of God means to you? Do you encourage other people to turn to the Bible? Buy several

Consider serving as a reader for gatherings outside of Mass: prayer services, retreats, meetings, or for people unable to come to Mass.

extra Bibles so you can give one away when you learn in conversation that someone doesn't own one. Would the chaplain's office at a local hospital or prison like to have a donation of Bibles or a volunteer who would read Scripture there?

Are there children who need special help? In local schools, are there pupils struggling to learn how to read? Would their teachers welcome a volunteer assistant? Do you have neighbors who have English as a second language? Are you patient with them, helping them to read and to speak?

Give some thought to the service of the Word. When you stand at the ambo, you want to be a person so completely imbued with the Word of God that it forms who you are, how you live, and how you serve other people.

Silence

The signature task of any reader is reading. But every reader must also be comfortable with silence. The GIRM (56) says, "The Liturgy of the Word is to be celebrated in such a way as to favor meditation, and so any kind of haste such as hinders recollection is clearly to be avoided."

We live in a busy culture. We rarely stop to think. We fill our empty spaces with noise and colors. We avoid the silence because silence makes us think, and thinking gives us insight, and insight may challenge us to live a different way, to rethink our values, to pick up a cross, and to follow Christ.

If you aspire to be a good reader, be good at silence. Make time each day to quiet your heart. Prepare yourself before you read. Use pauses while you read. The Word of God is truly present in the proclaimed Word. And the Spirit of God is truly present in the silences.

You have entered a holy place. You go up to the ambo to read. You center yourself. You experience God in your heart and in the community gathered before you. You open the lectionary. You see the words of Isaiah. All eyes are fixed on you. You take a breath. Rather, you take in the Breath. And you say, "The Spirit of the Lord is upon me."[3]

Questions for Discussion and Reflection

1. How do you use the Bible for prayer at home?

2. When have you experienced the power of God's Word to make a change in you—even a very small change?

3. Apart from the liturgy, how do you use the written word or the spoken word in service to others in your community?

4. When is the quietest part of your day? When is the noisiest?

---

3. See Luke 4:18.

Chapter Five

Frequently Asked Questions

1. What should I do if I make a mistake such as misspeaking a word or an entire line?

While good preparation helps us to cut down on errors, almost all readers have the experience of making a mistake at some point. If you realize the mistake immediately, it is generally best to pause slightly, restate the proper word or line, and go forward. It is never a good idea, however, to remark on or apologize for the error ("Oh, wait" or "I'm sorry") and then fix what you've said. If you simply correct the error and move on, people will understand and will remain focused on the text you are proclaiming, rather than on the fact that a mistake was made. If you are most of the way through the text or at the end, and realize a mistake was made, let it go.

No matter what happens, do not let a mistake at one point in the reading distract you from doing your best with the remainder of the reading. Taking a deep breath, focusing on where you are, and continuing to proclaim the reading well is the best way to "correct" any errors. Remembering also that most people will not recognize the mistake, and will simply listen to what you are proclaiming, can be very reassuring.

2. Our parish does not have a *Book of the Gospels*. Should we carry the lectionary in the opening procession?

No. If your parish does not have a *Book of the Gospels*, then no book is carried in the opening procession. In the same way, if there is no *Book of the Gospels,* the Gospel reader (deacon or priest) will bow to the altar in prayer, and then process to the ambo during the Gospel acclamation, without incense, candles, or servers.

3. How should the *Book of the Gospels* be placed on the altar?

The *Book of the Gospels* is often richly decorated and very expensive. We reverence the *Book of the Gospels* by carrying it in procession, placing it on the altar, and processing it to the ambo for the proclamation of the Gospel. It is not necessary or advisable to give reverence to the book by standing it up, open, on the altar, unless the parish has a stand that holds the book securely upright. Over time, this will pull the pages out of the binding and ruin a book that should last the church several generations. It is acceptable and correct to simply lay the book flat on the altar.

4. What if I am reading both the first and second reading? Should I stay at the ambo during the responsorial psalm or return to my seat?

Once a reading is finished, it is best to return to your seat, even if you are also doing the next reading. In many parishes, the cantor will come to the ambo to lead the psalm. Even if this is not the case for your parish, one of our roles as ministers is to help the assembly focus its attention on the center of the liturgy, and if you are not reading the psalm, you should be seated so that all can focus on the psalm rather than wonder why you are still at the ambo.

However, if you are reading both the first reading and the psalm, you should stay at the ambo, pause for at least fifteen to twenty seconds, and then begin the psalm rather than move back and forth.

5. Should I genuflect when I pass the tabernacle on my way to or from the ambo?

No. When the tabernacle is located in the sanctuary, the priest, deacon, and other ministers genuflect when they approach the altar (opening procession) and when they depart (closing procession), "but not during the celebration of Mass itself."[1] Indeed, moving to and from the ambo is a processional movement, and we do not genuflect in processions during the Mass.[2] The *Ceremonial of Bishops* states that "a deep bow is made to the altar by all who enter the sanctuary (chancel), leave it, or *pass before the altar*" (emphasis added).[3]

6. I understand that there is a three-year cycle of readings for Sundays. Why do I hear the same readings during Lent each year?

During the third, fourth, and fifth Sundays of Lent, many parishes will use the readings of year A each year. This is appropriate when there are members of the elect preparing for baptism at the Easter Vigil. The readings of year A are the basis for the "scrutinies" that the members of the elect undergo during these weeks. "The scrutinies are meant to uncover, then heal all that is weak, defective, or sinful in the hearts of the elect; to bring out, then strengthen all that is upright, strong, and good."[4]

7. What if I am assigned a reading that I am simply unable to proclaim well?

When you first know when you are scheduled to read, you should look at the readings you are assigned and come to some understanding of them. While some readings may be difficult to understand, complicated in their theology, or may be a "hard teaching" with which you are struggling, as readers we

---

1. GIRM, 274.
2. GIRM, 274.
3. RCIA, 141.
4. Ceremonial of Bishops, 72.

Reflecting on the Scripture readings before each Sunday Mass, even when you are not assigned, can help prepare you to step in if the assigned reader has not come.

should be willing to take on the challenge of spending time with those pieces and coming to an understanding of the text that we can express.

A reader will occasionally, though not very often, have difficulty publicly proclaiming a reading. If you pray with a reading and find that you just cannot proclaim it with meaning, let the coordinator of readers know, and find a substitute. However, this should be a personal call for you to spend more time with that reading and its context so that you can minister well the next time you are called on to read it.

8. What if I walk into church and am asked to fill in for a reader at that Mass?

Certainly readers always try to be as prepared as possible. But occasionally the unexpected intervenes, and you may be asked to read at a Mass when you did not expect it. Obviously, the vast majority of the preparation cannot be done in this case. Your regular preparation for Mass as a member of the assembly should include reading the Scriptures before coming to Mass, so that you will already have some familiarity with them. Whether or not that is the case, you can still take a prayerful moment to read through the passage before Mass and at least gain a basic sense of what you will be proclaiming. And if you are certain that you absolutely cannot do a decent job of proclaiming the Scripture in this situation, than you need to tell the priest celebrant or liturgy coordinator and ask that they find someone else to fill in.

9. What if my reading is not in the lectionary, or what if I need a larger size type than is in the lectionary?

For a variety of reasons, such as those named in the question, there may be times when your reading will need to be printed on a separate sheet and inserted into the lectionary or *Book of the Gospels*. This should be done before the Mass, in a way that will not damage the pages of the book. The page marker should be placed at this spot and the book opened and read as usual. The pages should not draw any special attention to themselves. At no time should you simply carry a piece of paper to the ambo to read from, nor should you pull one from your pocket and unfold it. To the assembly, the reading should appear as though from the book.

10. What if I arrive at church and discover that I have prepared the wrong reading?

A key challenge in this situation is to overcome your shock and dismay, and calm yourself so that you can use what short time you have to focus on studying the correct reading. As in question 8, you must simply do your best. Once past the experience, you should try to learn how the misunderstanding or miscommunication happened and talk with your coordinator about how to avoid it in the future.

11. What should I do if I return to the pew after my reading and discover that someone has taken my seat while I was reading?

Many readers have had the experience of getting up to read and finding that their seat has been taken quietly by a latecomer. If your parish has a good group of ushers, this is less likely to happen. If you don't have ushers, you could put a small RESERVED sign on your seat. But if it does happen, and you can see that there is no space for you as you leave the ambo, you should go to the side or back of the church rather than return to your seat.

Resources

Resources and Documents Related to Scripture and the Liturgy

Sacrosanctum concilium: The first document of the Second Vatican Council, promulgated on December 4, 1963, also known by its English title, *Constitution on the Sacred Liturgy*. It allowed the celebration of liturgical rites in the vernacular, called for the full, conscious, and active participation of the assembly, and ordered the revision of all liturgical rites.

Dei Verbum: This key document from the council, also known by its English title, *Dogmatic Constitution on Revelation*, has shaped much of the Church's understanding of sacred Scripture. Along with the *Constitution on the Sacred Liturgy*, it is foundational for the ministry of the Word.

General Instruction of the Roman Missal: The introductory document, or *praenotanda*, that explains the theological background and gives the directions for celebrating the Mass. It appears at the beginning of *The Roman Missal* and is published separately.

Ritual Books

National Conference of Catholic Bishops. *Lectionary for Mass for Use in the Dioceses of the United States of America*. 2nd typical ed.
    Vol. 1, Sundays, Solemnities, Feasts of the Lord and the Saints,
        Year A.
        Year B.
        Year C.
    Vol. 2, Weekdays, Year 1, Proper of Saints, Common of Saints.
    Vol. 3, Weekdays, Year 2, Proper of Saints, Common of Saints.
    Vol. 4, Common of Saints, Ritual Masses, Masses for Various Needs,
        Votive Masses, Masses for the Dead.

National Conference of Catholic Bishops. *Book of the Gospels for Use in the Dioceses of the United States of America*. Second Typical Edition.

The lectionary is the ritual book from which lectors and readers proclaim the readings at Mass. The *Book of the Gospels* is sometimes carried by a lector or reader if a deacon is not present.

Most Essential Pastoral Resources for
Reader Preparation (in order of usefulness)

Workbook for Lectors, Gospel Readers, and Proclaimers of the Word. Chicago: Liturgy Training Publications.

An essential week-by-week preparation tool for lectors and readers, this fundamental annual resource includes all Sundays of the year as well as the solemnities, feasts, and observances most attended in parishes. It is also helpful for priest celebrants, deacons, homilists, and those who prepare the liturgy. A copy given to each proclaimer of the Word promotes good proclamation and love of Scripture in the Sunday assembly. Readings are presented in large print and sense-line format—as they appear in the lectionary—to aid the reader in preparation, and lectionary numbers are included for each set of readings. The authors offer helpful commentaries for each reading, providing biblical and liturgical background information. Margin notes provide advice for effective pacing and expression and help with difficult pronunciations. Suggestions for words to stress are marked in the reading. Two editions are printed each year: one for churches in the United States with the NABRE translation of Scripture and another for churches in Canada with the NRSV translation of Scripture.

Prendergast, Michael R., Susan E. Meyers, and Timothy M. Milinovich. *Pronunciation Guide for the Lectionary: A Comprehensive Resource for Proclaimers of the Word.* Chicago: Liturgy Training Publications, 2009.

This is a straightforward little pronunciation guide that readers should have at home when they are preparing for their ministry. Any words that appear in the lectionary and have questionable or difficult pronunciations are included.

Lectionary for Mass, Sundays, Solemnities, Feasts of the Lord and Saints, Study Edition. Chicago: Liturgy Training Publications, 1970, 1998.

A paperback study edition of the first volume of the ritual edition of *The Lectionary for Mass*, this book will help readers become thoroughly familiar with the Sunday readings in all three cycles. It contains tables of readings and responsorial psalms as well as dates of all Sundays and feasts.

The Weekday Lectionary: Study Edition. Chicago: Liturgy Training Publications, 2002.

This convenient and comprehensive paperback volume contains all of the readings for weekday Masses, which are from the *New American Bible, Revised Edition* approved for use in the United States.

The Catholic Bible, Personal Study Edition: New American Bible. Jean Marie Heisberger, general editor. New York: Oxford University Press, 1995.

This is a terrific resource for anyone who is beginning to study the Scriptures. Features include a reading guide, discussion questions, background essays on aspects of Bible study, a glossary of specialized terms, full-color New Oxford Bible maps, and more. For the purposes of personally praying with, studying, and reflecting on the Scriptures, this is an excellent resource for all lectors.

The Catholic Study Bible: Third Edition. Donald Senior, John J. Collins, and Mary Ann Getty, editors. New York: Oxford University Press, 2010.

Readers will benefit from introductory essays on the historical, literary, and theological dimensions of Scripture and from abundant footnotes that provide historical explanations and clarify meaning. This Bible also includes an extensive reading guide for each book of the Bible, a concordance, indexes, helpful marginal references, and full-color maps.

Leal, Douglas. *Beyond Reading: Advanced Training for Proclaimers of the Word of God.* Chicago: Liturgy Training Publications, 2021.

There is a difference between reading God's Word and proclaiming it, between simply speaking words and bringing God's Word to life. From his many years of experience as a lector and lector trainer—and also as an actor and director—Douglas Leal knows how to coach lectors beyond reading, so that they can become proclaimers. Written in an informal, friendly style and organized in an orderly but lively format, this book provides ten coaching sessions and dozens of exercises to deepen the formation of committed proclaimers of the Word.

Sommers, Audrey. *Lector and Gospel Reader Workshop: A Resource for Bringing God's Word to Life.* Chicago: Liturgy Training Publications, 2006.

This resource is an interactive workshop on DVD for lectors and their trainers. The workshop combines the liturgical and spiritual aspects of being an effective lector with public speaking techniques. Participants will learn breathing exercises and will recite scriptural tongue twisters and word emphasis exercises before proclaiming a reading on camera for group critiques. The kit contains all instruction, promotion, and marketing materials needed in electronic form for a parish to have a successful workshop. It also provides prayers and handouts for home study.

Resources for Further Reader Preparation and Study

Brown, Raymond E., SS. *101 Questions and Answers on the Bible.* Mahwah, NJ: Paulist Press, 2003.

An accessible short reference by a renowned biblical scholar.

Frigge, Marielle, OSB. *Beginning Biblical Studies.* Winona, MN: Anselm Academic, 2013.

A clear, authoritative, inviting introduction to the Bible.

Hahn, Scott. *Catholic Bible Dictionary.* New York: Doubleday, 2009.

A useful and authoritative Bible dictionary.

New Collegeville Bible Commentary Series. Collegeville, MN: Liturgical Press.

Short booklets on individual books of the Bible, various dates.

New Jerome Commentary. Raymond E. Brown, Joseph A. Fitzmeyer, and Roland E. Murphy, eds. Upper Saddle River, New Jersey: Prentice Hall, 2008.

New Jerome Biblical Commentary is a line-by-line commentary on the Scriptures by Catholic biblical scholars. It is not an easy read, but it can explain many details in the content and context of a reading. A new edition was about to be published as this book went to press.

Paprocki, Joe. *The Bible Blueprint: A Catholic's Guide to Understanding and Embracing God's Word*. Chicago: Loyola Press, 2009.

This introduction for the novice is written by a popular and respected catechetical trainer.

LITURGY AND THE BIBLE SERIES

This series was designed especially for readers and other liturgical ministers who would like to be taught by scholars exceptional in their fields in brief books that are written in an inviting and lively style.

Bergant, Dianne, CSA. *O Lord, Open My Lips: The Psalms in the Liturgy*. Chicago: Liturgy Training Publications, 2018.

Biblical scholar Dianne Bergant explains how the psalms have nourished God's people through history and how they give us a voice in liturgy—Mass, sacraments, Liturgy of the Hours and liturgies of the Word.

Boisclair, Regina A. *The Word of the Lord at Mass: Understanding the Lectionary*. Chicago, Liturgy Training Publications, 2015.

Professor Regina Boisclair, an expert on the lectionary, explains what the lectionary is, how it was designed, how its arrangement generates theological insights, and how all its marvelous parts move together through the liturgical year.

Cameron, Michael. *Unfolding Sacred Scripture: How Catholics Read the Bible*. Chicago: Liturgy Training Publications, 2015.

Professor of early Christianity and Scripture Michael Cameron invites readers into the Catholic practice of reading Scripture, first explaining the Church's understanding of the Bible and ways of interpreting it, and then providing a brief guided tour through the major parts and essential themes of the Bible.

Clifford, Richard J. *Thus Says the Lord: The Prophets in the Liturgy*. Chicago, Liturgy Training Publications, 2021.

Biblical scholar Richard Clifford shares his knowledge and insights on the ancient work of prophecy in the near east, the biblical prophets, the role of the prophetic books in the Bible (focusing especially on Isaiah), and how the prophets' words function for us in the liturgy.

Senior, Donald, CP. *Composing Sacred Scripture: How the Bible Was Formed*. Chicago: Liturgy Training Publications, 2016.

Scripture scholar Donald Senior describes how the texts of the Bible came to be. He shares the origin stories of all the diverse parts that make up what we know as the Bible, how all the parts came together, and how Christians have come to understand them as inspired and true.

Resources for Prayer and Reflection

At Home with the Word®. Chicago: Liturgy Training Publications.

> Prepare to listen to God's Word each Sunday, at home alone or with a group. It contains the texts of the Sunday readings for the particular year (year A, B, or C), the responsorial psalms, and Scripture reflections with questions for study and discussion, as well as meditations on the practice of virtue. It uses the NABRE Scripture texts from the *Lectionary for Mass* for the United States and is also available in large print and in a Spanish-language version titled *Palabra de Dios*.

Casey, Michael. *Sacred Reading: The Ancient Art of Lectio Divina*. Liguori, MS: Liguori, 1997.

> This is an accessible but profound book about the practice of lectio divina that will nourish readers in their ministry.

Daily Prayer. Chicago: Liturgy Training Publications.

> This annual resource provides an order of prayer for each day of the liturgical year. Using a familiar order of prayer, it enables further reflection on the sacred mysteries celebrated in the liturgy. The Gospel of the day from the daily Mass is provided, and the prayer texts and reflections are in tune with the observance of the seasons, solemnities, feasts of the Lord, and commemoration of saints celebrated during the liturgical year.

Magrassi, Mariano, OSB. *Praying the Bible: An Introduction to* Lectio Divina. Translated by Edward Hagman, OFM CAP. Collegeville, MN: Liturgical Press, 1998.

> The author begins with the proclamation of Scripture in the liturgy, showing how private prayerful reading of Scripture *(lectio divina)* and communal prayerful hearing of Scripture are two inseparable practices that nourish each other. Providing rich insights from early Church writers on the role of Scripture in the spiritual life as well as their advice on developing the disposition for *lectio divina,* this book offers an inspiring and fortifying initiation into an ancient practice that will be especially helpful for readers.

Shea, John. *The Spiritual Wisdom of the Gospels for Christian Preachers and Teachers*. Collegeville, MN: Liturgical Press.

> In each volume you'll find spiritual wisdom from John Shea for each Gospel reading—first a spiritual commentary and then a teaching that flows from the commentary.

> *Matthew, year A, On Earth As It Is in Heaven*, 2004.
>
> *Mark, year B, Eating with the Bridegroom*, 2005.
>
> *Luke, year C, The Relentless Widow*, 2006.
>
> *Feasts, Funerals, Weddings, Following Love into Mystery*, 2010.

Websites

New American Bible: Revised Edition and lectionary readings: www.usccb.org
/bible; https://bible.usccb.org/bible/readings/

At the first url, the United States Conference of Catholic Bishops provides the New
American Bible: Revised Edition in electronic form. The second address takes you to
the lectionary reading of the day with an option to move forward and backward in the
calendar using arrows.

Toastmasters International: www.toastmasters.org/

This website provides resources for improving public speaking and can help with
some skills a lector needs.

Glossary

Alb: A full-length white liturgical robe, from the Latin *albus*, meaning "white." The alb is the preferred vestment for all ministers, from server to bishop. It recalls the white garment put on at baptism as a sign of putting on the new life of Christ. Ordained ministers wear a stole and an outer garment over the alb. In some churches, on some occasions, readers are sometimes vested in an alb.

Altar: The sacred table on which the sacrifice of the Mass is celebrated. It is the central symbol of Christ in a church building. In the United States, the table of the altar may be made of stone or wood; the base or supports may be made of any dignified and solid material. In new churches there is to be only one altar. When passing the altar to go to the ambo to proclaim their assigned reading, readers make a profound bow.

Ambo: A dignified and stationary place from which the readings, responsorial psalm, and Easter proclamation are to be proclaimed. It may also be used for giving the homily and for announcing the intentions of the prayer of the faithful. The term is derived from a Greek word for "raised place."

Amen: Hebrew word meaning "so be it." It is a response of the assembly indicating agreement or assent. The Great Amen is the concluding acclamation to the Eucharistic Prayer.

Apocalyptic: From a Greek word meaning "unveiling" or "revelation." In Christian usage it refers to the Book of Revelation (also called the Apocalypse), the final book of the Bible, and images or writings based on its visions of the end of the world and the fulfillment of all creation in a new heaven and a new earth (Revelation 21:1).

Assembly: The people gathered for divine worship, often called the congregation. The *Constitution on the Sacred Liturgy* (no. 7), discussing the many ways Christ is present in the sacrifice of the Mass, says, "He is present . . . when the church prays and sings, for he promised: 'Where two or three are gathered together in my name, there am I in the midst of them' (Matthew 18:20)." Contemporary liturgical theology emphasizes that it is the assembly as a whole that celebrates the liturgy under the leadership of a priest.

Bible: The fundamental book of religious writings of the Judeo-Christian tradition. The psalms from the Old Testament were the original hymnal for both Jewish and Christian worship. Sung and proclaimed sections from the Bible form a major part of every worship service.

Book of the Gospels: A ritual book from which the passages from the Gospels prescribed for Masses on Sundays, solemnities, feasts of the Lord and of the saints, and ritual masses are proclaimed; also called an *evangeliary*. It may be carried in the entrance procession and placed on the altar, and then processed to the ambo during the Gospel acclamation. It is presented to deacons at their ordination and held over the heads of bishops at their ordination.

Deacon: An ordained minister of the Catholic Church belonging to the first of the three orders of ordained ministry that may be received through the sacrament of holy orders: deacon, priest, and bishop. Deacons are ordained for the service of charity in the world as well as for liturgical ministry. Their liturgical duties at Mass include proclaiming the Gospel, announcing the intentions of the universal prayer, assisting the priest at the altar, administering the Precious Blood to the faithful, and dismissing the people at the end of Mass.

Discourse: A speech, lecture, or letter that makes an argument or explanation.

Genres: Literary types that have a characteristic style, form, and subject matter.

Gospel: The good news of Jesus Christ. The term *Gospel* usually refers to one of the four accounts of the life, death, and resurrection of Jesus found in the Bible, ascribed to Matthew, Mark, Luke, and John.

Gospel Acclamation: The title given to the rite within the celebration of Mass that greets the Lord, who is about to speak to the assembly in the Gospel, and prepares the assembly for its proclamation. The Gospel acclamation consists of the Alleluia (or, during Lent, other words of praise) sung by all, followed by a verse (frequently from Scripture) sung by a cantor or by a choir, and then the refrain sung again by all. Several verses may be used to cover the action of a Gospel procession.

Lectio Divina: A process of slow meditation on the Word of God.

Lectionary for Mass: A four-volume series that contains the readings (including the responsorial psalms) for each day of the year—for Sundays, weekdays, and various needs and occasions.

Lectio Continua: The continuous reading of Scripture at Mass and in the Office of Readings in the Liturgy of the Hours. It is an ancient tradition to read from Scripture in a continuous or semicontinuous manner, beginning one day where the previous day's reading ended. This tradition is followed for the most part in the Sunday and weekday lectionary cycles.

Lector: Although the title is frequently applied to any reader, a lector is a lay reader who has been "instituted" in a ceremony by a bishop to read from the lectionary at Mass.

Liturgy of the Eucharist: The third part of the Mass that begins with the preparation of the gifts and ends with the prayer after Communion, during which the action of the Mass is centered around the altar.

Liturgy of the Word: The second part of the Mass that begins at the first reading and ends after the prayer of the faithful, during which the action of the Mass is centered around the ambo.

Narrative: A story.

Proclamation: The act of proclaiming—that is, the act of making known publicly. Within the context of the role of the reader, proclamation is the act of making known to the gathered assembly "the continuity of the work of salvation according to God's wonderful design."[1]

Profound Bow: A gesture that "signifies reverence and honor shown to the persons themselves or to the signs that represent them."[2] A profound bow is generally made from the waist. In the liturgy, profound bows are made by the celebrant to the altar, during the prayer *Munda cor meum* ("Almighty God, cleanse my heart . . .") and *In spiritu humilitatis* ("With humble spirit . . ."), in the Creed at the words *Et incarnatus est* ("by the power of the Holy Spirit . . . and became man"—in this instance, *all* bow), and in the Roman Canon at the words *Supplices te rogamus* ("In hummble prayer we ask you, almighty God"). The same kind of bow is made by the deacon when he asks for a blessing before the proclamation of the Gospel. In addition, the priest bows slightly as he speaks the words of the Lord at the consecration.[3]

Table of the Lord: A term sometimes used to refer to the altar. Patristic texts also see the ambo as being a symbolic table, however, and in liturgical writing reference is often made to the "two tables"—or the table of the Word of God and the table of the Body of Christ (see *Constitution on the Sacred Liturgy*, 48, 51).

Theme: A topic or subject matter.

---

1. GIRM, 357.
2. GIRM, 275.
3. GIRM, 275b.

Prayer for Readers

R. Speak, Lord, for your servant is listening.　　　　1 Samuel 3:9

> Blessed are you, O Lord;
> 　　teach me your statutes.
> With my lips I recite
> 　　all the judgments you have spoken.　　Psalm 119:12–13

R. Speak, Lord, for your servant is listening.　　　　1 Samuel 3:9

> In your statutes I take delight;
> 　　I will never forget your word.
> I cling to your testimonies, Lord;
> 　　Do not let me come to shame.　　Psalm 119:16, 31

R. Speak, Lord, for your servant is listening.　　　　1 Samuel 3:9

> I will run the way of your commandments,
> 　　for you will broaden my heart.
> I lift up my hands to your commandments;
> 　　I study your statutes, which I love.　　Psalm 119:32, 48

R. Speak, Lord, for your servant is listening.　　　　1 Samuel 3:9

> Teach me wisdom and knowledge
> 　　For in your commandments I trust.　　Psalm 119:66
>
> How I love your law, Lord!
> 　　I study it all day long.　　Psalm 119:66; 97

R. Speak, Lord, for your servant is listening.　　　　1 Samuel 3:9

> How sweet to my tongue is your promise,
> 　　sweeter than honey to my mouth!
> Your word is a lamp for my feet,
> 　　a light for my path,　　Psalm 119:103, 105

R. Speak, Lord, for your servant is listening.　　　　1 Samuel 3:9

> I make a solemn vow
> 　　to observe your righteous judgments.
> May my lips pour forth your praise,
> 　　because you teach me your statues.
> May my tongue sing of your promise,
> 　　for all your commandments are righteous.　　Psalm 119:106, 171–172

R. Speak, Lord, for your servant is listening.　　　　1 Samuel 3:9